1x(²/₁₃)³/₁₅
1X. 9/15. ¹¹/₁₄
1X₀ 8/17. 3/18

D1442616

Australia

New and Future Titles in the Indigenous Peoples of the World Include:

Gypsies
Pacific Islands
Southeast Asia

Indigenous Peoples of the World

Australia

Anne Wallace Sharp

LUCENT BOOKS
SAN DIEGO, CALIFORNIA

THOMSON
GALE

Detroit • New York • San Diego • San Francisco
Boston • New Haven, Conn. • Waterville, Maine
London • Munich

Library of Congress Cataloging-in-Publication Data

Sharp, Anne Wallace.
    Australia / by Anne Wallace Sharp.
        p. cm. — (Indigenous peoples of the world)
Summary: Discusses the historical origins, beliefs, arts, family life, cultural clashes with whites, and future hopes of the aboriginal people of
Australia.
    Includes bibliographical references and index.
    ISBN 1-59018-091-7 (hard : alk. paper)
    1. Australian aborigines—History—Juvenile literature. 2. Australian
aborigines—Social life and customs—Juvenile literature. [1. Australian
aborigines.] I. Title. II. Indigenous peoples of the world.
  GN665 .S523 2003
  305.89' 915—dc21

2002000457

Contents

Foreword

Nearly every area of the world has indigenous populations, those people who are descended from the original settlers of a given region, often arriving many millennia ago. Many of these populations exist today despite overwhelming odds against their continuing survival.

Though indigenous populations have come under attack for a variety of reasons, in most cases land lies at the heart of the conflict. The hunger for land has threatened indigenous societies throughout history, whether the aggressor was a neighboring tribe or a foreign culture. The reason for this is simple: For indigenous populations, *way of life* has nearly always depended on the land and its bounty. Indeed, cultures from the Inuit of the frigid Arctic to the Yanomami of the torrid Amazon rain forest have been indelibly shaped by the climate and geography of the regions they inhabit.

As newcomers moved into already settled areas of the world, competition led to tension and violence. When newcomers possessed some important advantage—greater numbers or more powerful weapons—the results were predictable. History is rife with examples of outsiders triumphing over indigenous populations. Anglo-Saxons and Vikings, for instance, moved into eastern Europe and the British Isles at the expense of the indigenous Celts. Europeans traveled south through Africa and into Australia displacing the indigenous Bushmen and Aborigines while other Westerners ventured into the Pacific at the expense of the indigenous Melanesians, Micronesians, and Polynesians. And in North and South America, the colonization of the New World by European powers resulted in the decimation and displacement of numerous Native American groups.

Nevertheless, many indigenous populations retained their identity and managed to survive. Only in the last one hundred years, however, have anthropologists begun to study with any objectivity the hundreds of indigenous societies found throughout the world. And only within the last few decades have these societies been truly appreciated and acknowledged for their richness and complexity. The ability to adapt to and manage their environments is but one marker of the incredible resourcefulness of many indigenous populations. The Inuit, for example, created two distinct modes of travel for getting around the barren, icy region that is their home. The sleek, speedy kayak—with its whalebone frame and sealskin cover—allowed the Inuit to silently skim the waters of the nearby ocean and bays. And the sledge (or dogsled)—with its caribou hide platform and runners built from whalebone or frozen fish covered with sealskin—made travel over the snow- and ice-covered landscape possible.

The Indigenous Peoples of the World series strives to present a clear and realistic picture of the world's many and varied native cultures. The series captures the uniqueness as well as the similarities of indigenous societies by examining family and community life, traditional spirituality and religion, warfare, adaptation to the environment, and interaction with other native and nonnative peoples.

The series also offers perspective on the effects of Western civilization on indigenous populations as well as a multifaceted view of contemporary life. Many indigenous societies, for instance, struggle today with poverty, unemployment, racism, poor health, and a lack of educational opportunities. Others find themselves embroiled in political instability, civil unrest, and violence. Despite the problems facing these societies, many indigenous populations have regained a sense of pride in them-

selves and their heritage. Many also have experienced a resurgence of traditional art and culture as they seek to find a place for themselves in the modern world.

The Indigenous Peoples of the World series offers an in-depth study of different regions of the world and the people who have long inhabited those regions. All books in the series include fully documented primary and secondary source quotations that enliven the text. Sidebars highlight notable events, personalities, and traditions, while annotated bibliographies offer ideas for future research. Numerous maps and photographs provide the reader with a pictorial glimpse of each society.

From the Aborigines of Australia to the various indigenous peoples of the Caribbean, Europe, South America, Mexico, Asia, and Africa, the series covers a multitude of societies and their cultures. Each book stands alone and the series as a collection offers valuable comparisons of the past history and future problems of the indigenous peoples of the world.

Who Are the Indigenous People of Australia?

Australia is the only country on earth that is also a continent. Some of the most unusual plants and animals in the world can be found there. A unique and fascinating place, Australia is also the home of the Aborigines, who are, according to Aboriginal historians, "the oldest living culture in the world."[1]

The Aborigines are the indigenous, or native, people of Australia. The word "Aborigine" comes from the Latin phrase *"ab origine"* meaning "from the beginning." When spelled with a small "a," the word refers to any people whose ancestors were the first to live in a country; but when spelled with a capital "A," the word refers only to the native people of Australia.

For centuries the Aborigines led a semi-nomadic life, moving around the continent of Australia as the climate and the seasons changed. Until relatively recently they did not grow crops, use metals, or make pottery. They built no towns or roads, had no written language, and maintained extensive trading networks without benefit of wheeled equipment or vehicles. Most made homes in temporary bark or brush huts and lived off the land. Yet despite many years of cruel and insensitive treatment, the indigenous people of Australia have survived and much of their culture has been kept alive.

This primitive lifestyle blinded Europeans to the rich culture the Aborigines had developed. Indeed, governments, missionaries, and settlers alike attempted to eradicate the Aboriginal way of life.

In the Beginning

The Aborigines first arrived in Australia some fifty to sixty-five thousand years ago. They traveled to Australia from Asia and Indonesia in one of history's great migrations. The Aborigines migrated at a time when earth was much cooler than it is today and the world looked much different. An ice age had locked away a lot of the planet's oceans in mile-thick ice sheets that covered much of the Northern Hemisphere. This resulted in a much lower sea level, making it possible for the Aborigines to walk across land bridges that no longer exist today.

No one knows for sure why these people migrated south. Some historians think that they were pushed out of Asia and Indonesia by stronger tribes to the north. Others believe that they were simply in search of new hunting lands. For whatever reason, the people who would become the Aborigines decided to make the move and ended up on the continent of Australia.

When they reached Australia, the Aborigines scattered themselves widely across the continent, becoming its first human occupants. Scientists estimate that it took the natives perhaps ten thousand years to explore and settle the entire country, so that by around forty thousand years ago, most parts of Australia were occupied. During this time the Ice Age ended and the land bridges vanished, leaving the Aborigines isolated and stranded on the island continent.

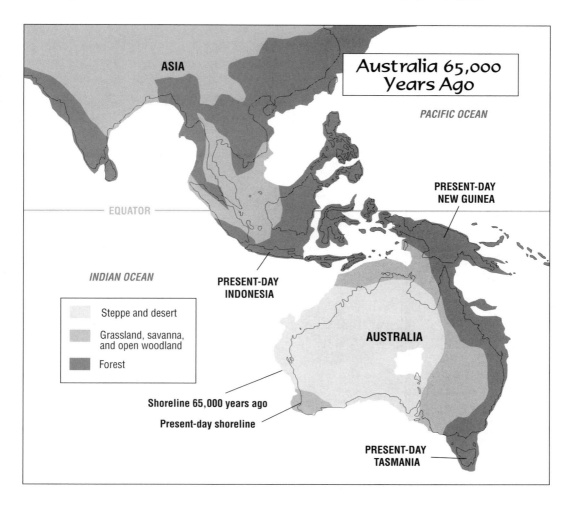

ASIA

Australia 65,000 Years Ago

PACIFIC OCEAN

PRESENT-DAY NEW GUINEA

EQUATOR

INDIAN OCEAN

PRESENT-DAY INDONESIA

Steppe and desert

Grassland, savanna, and open woodland

Forest

AUSTRALIA

Shoreline 65,000 years ago

Present-day shoreline

PRESENT-DAY TASMANIA

The different kinds of land within Australia meant that there were great differences in Aboriginal lifestyles from region to region. Never one united people, the Aborigines lived in clans and tribes but had no chiefs. Each group of natives had its own language and its own rituals, although the Aborigines' basic way of life and beliefs were quite similar throughout the continent.

A Brief History

Living peacefully off the land, the Aborigines grew in population to an estimated 1 million until a hot summer day in 1788 when a fleet of English ships sailed into what is today Sydney Harbor. As it did in North America, the arrival of Europeans in Australia brought devastating changes to the native culture. Many Aborigines were killed or forced from their homes by the settlers and were separated from their families. Entire groups of Aborigines died from diseases introduced by the Europeans.

During the more than two hundred years since the white "invasion" of Australia, the Aborigines have struggled to survive and maintain their rich cultural and spiritual heritage. Today around

A young Aborigine boy in ceremonial paint playing with a toy gun personifies the influences of both past and present on Australia's indigenous culture.

257,000 Aborigines live in Australia, mostly in rural communities and isolated settlements, making up approximately 2 percent of the total population of the country. They live on the fringes of society and are fighting to gain a solid place in the Australian mainstream.

As the twenty-first century begins, the Aborigines suffer many of the same problems facing Native Americans. They lag far behind whites in education, employment, and health care. They also struggle with racism, alcoholism, and poverty. And yet despite overwhelming odds, the Aborigines of Australia have made significant advances in the last twenty years and look to the future with hope and optimism.

The unique and rich Australian Aboriginal culture, long ignored and suppressed, is now experiencing an exciting renewal. The real story of Australia's history and its indigenous people is for the first time beginning to be known and celebrated.

Chapter 1

The Land and Its Resources

Living in Australia has always been a challenge. As the Aborigines moved across the landscape during the years of their settlement, they found a harsh land, unusual animals, and wide variations in climate and environment. In order to survive in this land, the Aborigines were forced to adapt to the extremes and make use of every animal and plant they found. According to writer Bill Bryson, "No people on earth have lived in more environments with greater success."[2]

The Continent of Australia

Australia is made up of two islands—the mainland and the smaller island of Tasmania, which lies to the south. These two islands were once joined together but split apart thousands of years ago. Today Australia is divided into seven vast states and one small territory. The states are New South Wales, Tasmania, Victoria, Queensland, Western Australia, South Australia, and the Northern Territory. The capital city of Canberra is located in a metro-sized region lacking statehood status, called the Australian Capital Territory.

Australia is often referred to as "the Land Down Under" because it lies entirely within the Southern Hemisphere. Being in the Southern Hemisphere makes everything "backward" in Australia. When it is winter in North America, for instance, it is summer in Australia.

The name "Australia" comes from the Latin word *Australis,* which simply means "southern." Lying between the Indian and Pacific Oceans, half of Australia lies in the earth's tropical zone. The Tropics are a broad band of land just north and south of the equator that include some of the hottest areas on earth.

The Outback

The word "Outback" can be applied to nearly two-thirds of Australia and is generally understood to mean the largely uninhabited interior of the continent. Despite its immense size, only 15 percent of Australians live in the Outback. Those individuals who do reside there usually live in isolated homesteads or settlements where the majority are engaged in some form of farming. Residents of the Outback like to refer to their homeland as the "Never-Never."

Flat plains, desert, and some of the most unusual rock formations on the planet characterize the Outback. The soil is rust red in color and is responsible for the area's nickname—the Red Center. Much of the Outback is covered with beach grass, or spinifex, which is knife-sharp and has barbs on the blades similar to cactus tips. Long droughts are common, as is extreme heat. Temperatures of over 110 degrees are not unusual, although the overnight temperatures, even in the deserts, can drop into the teens.

In fact, the interior of Australia is so hot that one town there—Coober Pedy—has been built primarily underground. The oldest and largest opal mining town in

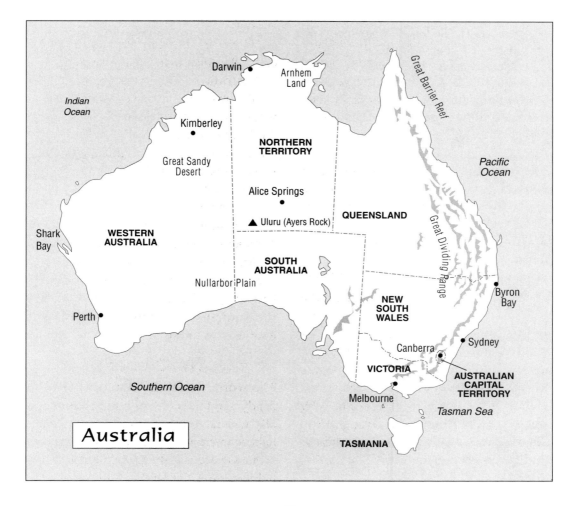

Finding Shelter

Finding shelter—shelter from the intense heat of the daytime and the cold nights—was essential for the natives of Australia. The Aborigines built no permanent dwellings nor did they make tents. Instead, they used whatever they could find on the landscape.

Many tribes utilized the numerous sandstone caves that dotted the country, while others built temporary shelters made of bark, called *humpies, wurlies, wilchas,* or *gunyahs.* These small makeshift huts were formed with large pieces of bark and branches that were then laced together with grass strings. The homes were primitive, simple, and easily built, and they provided a comfortable shelter in all weather. During the cold winter months, the Aborigines slept close together for warmth around a fire in the middle of their dwellings.

During the summer months, the Aborigines much preferred to sleep outside. In fact, even today many Aborigines who have modern housing choose to sleep outside during warm weather, using their wooden homes as large storage areas. It is only during the winter that these twenty-first-century Aborigines move inside.

Australia, Coober Pedy is an amazing place. Hotels, stores, restaurants, and houses are all underground, as the residents there have discovered that this offers them the best form of protection from the unbearable heat.

Finding Water

In this hot climate, the most important survival skill for the Aborigines was the ability to find water. Because of the dryness and lack of rain, water holes, or billabongs, were few and far between. With few rivers and lakes to rely upon, the Aborigines were forced to learn how to find water where none was visible from a distance.

Sometimes they would lie down on the sand and listen for the sound of water underground. They also learned how to scan the horizon and find distant water by using their keen eyesight to discern the vague shimmering of heat vapors above the land that indicated nearby water. Their sense of smell was so acute that many natives were also able to locate water by a faint whiff of odor in the air.

The Aborigines soon realized that certain plants contain water in their roots, so the natives made wide use of these resources as well. The Aborigines also discovered a kind of frog that contains sacs of water in its body. They quickly acquired the skill to find these creatures deep beneath the dry lake beds.

Clothing

Throughout their history the Aborigines have worn little or no clothing. The vast majority of early natives chose to be naked. According to writer James Cowan, "For the Aborigine, clothing his body . . . destroy[ed] the relationship he enjoy[ed] with his land . . . since it separate[d] him from what he [was]." Instead of relying on clothing, the Aborigines preferred to decorate their bodies with various paints and tattoos. This body decoration, Cowan explains, "reaffirm[ed] his/her relationship with the sacred nature of the clan's coun-

try."[3] To keep the skin from overexposure to bugs and sunlight, the Aborigines often coated their bodies with a mixture of ocher (paint), fat from animals, and various plant juices.

Those Aboriginal men who did wear clothing wore a *naga,* or loincloth, and nothing else, while women wore a simple "minidress" that barely covered them. These were made from animal skins. Children usually went around naked. The Aborigines also went barefoot except for a sandal-like shoe that was sometimes used while traveling through the hot deserts of the interior. In colder areas, both men and

By using earth-based paints instead of clothing to cover their bodies, Aborigines reaffirm their close bond to the land.

women wore capelike garments made of kangaroo skin. This clothing was tied over the shoulders or around the neck in an effort to keep the arms free for movement. In some cases, possum fur was substituted for kangaroo skin.

In modern Australia many Aborigines wear Western clothing such as jeans and T-shirts on a daily basis. A few tribes who live in the ancient way still "dress" as their ancestors did. On ceremonial occasions or on sacred journeys to the Outback, most Aborigines revert to the nonclothing of the past.

Tools for Survival

The Aborigines developed a wide range of special tools to enable them to survive in the hostile environments of Australia. Most of the tools were simple in design and made of stone, wood, or bone. Digging sticks were used to dig up vegetables and also were helpful in catching snakes and lizards and in opening up the huge termite mounds that dotted the Outback of Australia. The Aborigines also made simple axes and cutting tools for use in the carving and chopping of wood.

Grinding stones were used to prepare seeds and nuts for eating. Bones from various animals came in handy for needles, while scooped-out pieces of wood were fashioned into dishes and cooking utensils. Food for the winter was often stored in containers made of wood, bark, and woven fibers.

Bush Tucker and Cooking

Bush tucker is the name used by white Australians for all the different kinds of food that the Aborigines have been eating for thousands of years. According to Aboriginal historians, "The countryside was like a huge supermarket where the Aboriginal people could browse at will, picking and choosing what to eat and when to eat it. Everything they ate and drank was beneficial to the body."[4]

The Aborigines, for instance, collected many different kinds of seeds. The seeds from various wild grains and plants were ground between two stones and used as a kind of flour. Water was then added to make bread, or *damper*. This mixture was placed in the ashes of a fire for cooking. Many Aborigines used the bark from a paperbark tree to make "ground ovens." The natives started by placing hot rocks in a hole, covering them with paperbark leaves, and adding water. Meat was placed in this primitive oven and covered with more leaves, allowing the meat to cook slowly until done.

The Use of Plants as Food

Plants, usually gathered by women, were used extensively by all Aborigines and formed the bulk of their diet. Along the coast the natives made wide use of such delicacies as cabbage palm, sea almond, mangrove seeds, tropical coconuts, plums, and figs.

Wild tomatoes (*wamulu*), bush raisins, and wild onions (*minyarra*) were favored by the Aborigines who lived in the desert regions of Australia. In desert regions the Aborigines' main source of nutrients was the yam. Also called a wild potato, or *cun-*

manggu, this vegetable tastes like a sweet potato and was either eaten raw or cooked in hot coals.

A real favorite in northern Queensland was a special dish called *kup maori.* This meal consisted of meat and vegetables wrapped in banana leaves and then roasted in an underground oven.

The baobab tree is instantly recognizable in the Australian Outback. It has a grotesque appearance and can live for thousands of years. With a massive trunk and small spindly branches, the tree bears fruit that has, for centuries, provided the Aborigines with vitamin C and protein.

Eating Insects

The Aborigines, in their effort to find every valuable source of food, also made wide use of various insects. Like many other native groups around the world, the Aborigines ate grubs, moths, ants, bees,

The Use of Fire

Early in their history, the Aborigines learned to make fire by rubbing two sticks together until a flame burst forth. Fire was essential to the natives. They used it to roast meat, keep insects away, send messages, warm their nights, and ward off animals. Fire was also used to drive small animals such as kangaroos and wallabies into position for easy hunting. To accomplish this, the Aborigines made a large circle of fire with only one exit. The animals were then driven inside, where hunters could more easily kill them.

Fire making was uniquely the responsibility of Aboriginal men. Campfires were often kept burning around the clock, and when the tribe traveled, live fire sticks were carried from one site to the next.

One of the most important uses of fire was to renew the land. The Aborigines of Australia employed a special technique called firestick farming to accomplish this. The natives regularly burned off bushes, grasses, and undergrowth in order to maintain the grasslands. Ashes from the fires fertilized the soil and provided an opportunity for the growth of fresh green plants. This, in turn, attracted more animals for hunting. The result was a thick and rich new crop of grass that sprouted after the rains came.

Modern scientists widely believe that this practice changed the landscape of Australia. In the process, fire-adapted plants and animals had a better chance of survival. Australians no longer use firestick farming, and many scientists are quick to point out that this has resulted in an actual decrease in the survival rates of many plants and animals.

and other insects, which supplied a wealth of nutrients and vitamins.

Witchety grubs were one of the most important insects consumed by the Aborigines. These grubs, or larvae, are found in the roots of the witchety bush, or acacia, in central Australia. Women collected these insects by digging up the bush and then collecting the grubs that were found hidden in the roots. The witchety grub is nearly three inches long, ivory in color, and covered with fine hairs. When the head is removed after cooking, a soft custardlike mass oozes out.

According to biologist Ron Cherry, "The grubs can be eaten raw or can be cooked in ashes. Cooking causes the grub to swell. . . . Cooked witchety grubs have been [said] to taste like almonds. The larvae are rich in calories, protein, and fat. Ten large grubs are sufficient to provide for the daily needs of an adult male."[5] When crushed, witchety grubs were also used as a protective ointment and covering for wounds and burns.

Another insect that provided nutrition for the Aborigines was the ant. Some species of ants are rich in a honey-like material that provided a source of sugar for the natives. The green ant, while not containing this special "honey," is flavored, instead, like lemons. The Aborigines frequently dug up the ants' nest,

scrunched it up, and mixed the resulting powder with water to create a liquid that was used for treating the common cold.

Another popular "sugary" food source was the honeybag, or hive, of the stingless Australian bee. To locate this honeybag, the Aborigines "caught" a bee feeding on pollen and attached a small leaf to it by using sticky plant juices. When the insect was released, the natives followed the bee straight to the hive. A stick could then be poked into the hive until the honey ran down the stick into a bark basket.

An Aborigine child with witchety grubs, insect larvae found in the roots of the witchety plant. The grubs are an important source of food for Aborigines.

Fishing

For those Aborigines who lived along the coast, special devices were used for catching fish and other marine animals. In southeast Australia, for instance, the natives made eel traps out of twined plant fibers. They also used a complicated system of dams, channels, and pens to trap fish and eels. These dams were usually made out of stone and enabled the natives to catch the fish more easily.

Many of the Aborigines fished from simple canoes and rafts. Long pieces of bark were tied together using tree vines. The Iora tribe, who lived in New South Wales, fished from canoes made out of eucalyptus wood. While not as stable or as well made as the birch canoes used by Native Americans, these canoes served the Aborigines well. The vessels were easy to carry and could be quickly built. This made life simpler for the Iora, who seldom stayed in one area for more than a few weeks.

The Darak tribe near Sydney also relied on the sea for its livelihood. The women made fishing lines from bark fiber and created hooks out of various seashells. Because the hooks were brittle and tended to break off in a fish's mouth, the Daraks always fished in pairs. A woman carefully pulled the hooked fish to shore, where a man stood ready to spear it.

Coastal Aborigines also hunted the dugong, or sea cow. Weighing around a thousand pounds and over ten feet long, the dugong is gray in color and has a rounded head, small eyes, and large snout. Dugongs are cousins to the manatees found in Florida rivers.

The Eating of Kangaroos and Marsupials

Kangaroos formed a large part of the Aboriginal diet, as did other marsupial animals. Marsupials, with a few exceptions (like the opossum of North America), are found only in Australia. When the continent of Australia became isolated thousands of years ago, its animals were stranded and evolved in different ways than their relatives elsewhere. As a result, many of the animals long resident in Australia are found nowhere else in the world.

Marsupials are members of the mammal family: They are warm-blooded, have body hair, and feed their offspring with breast milk—all characteristics of mammals. And yet marsupials are also quite different from other mammals because of two unique characteristics. First of all, they give birth to babies that are not fully formed. At birth, for instance, a baby kangaroo's body is only about a half-inch long. Despite its tiny size, the baby is able to pull its way up its mother's fur and into a pouch. Pouches on female animals, the

The Bogong Moth

One of the most interesting insects the Aborigines used for food was the Bogong moth. These moths are found in only one place—Mount Bogong of New South Wales. Every year from November to January, hundreds of Aborigines from dozens of different tribes journeyed to the mountains to collect and feast upon these insects.

The adult moths tend to gather in rock crevices throughout the mountains. Some of the rocks are literally covered with layer after layer of moths. These congregations made it easy for the Aborigines to dislodge and collect the insects in large woven baskets.

Once collected, the moths were cooked in sand and stirred in hot ashes. This cooking process singed off the moth's legs and wings. After removing the insect's head, the Aborigines ate the moth, which was extremely rich in fat. At other times the moths were ground into a paste and made into cakes.

second unique trait, are probably the best known characteristic of marsupials, who derive their name from the Latin word *marsupium,* which means "pouch."

The kangaroo is one of the national symbols of Australia. Coming in many sizes and shapes, there are over fifty different kangaroo species. The largest is the red kangaroo, which can reach nearly seven feet tall and weigh up to two hundred pounds. The smallest is the tiny hopping mouse kangaroo, which is only two inches tall.

Kangaroo tail soup is still considered a delicacy among the Aborigines of the twenty-first century. The stew consists of kangaroo flesh, onions, carrots, and potatoes. In earlier times the kangaroo was hunted down, killed with a boomerang, and then thrown straight onto a fire and cooked in its juices. The meat was eaten slightly raw.

Weapons for Hunting— the Boomerang

The Aborigines invented the boomerang, a remarkable weapon that greatly improved their hunting. Originally the crescent-shaped implement was carved from wood, which was usually painted with animals and other designs.

Some boomerangs return to the thrower while others do not. The boomerang used by the Aborigines for hunting was of the kind that did not return to the thrower, while the returning type was used only in traditional native sports and games. Cultures in India and Egypt also used a similar weapon, but only the Australian Aborigines had one that returned.

The boomerang, when thrown correctly, was able to accurately hit an animal and then bounce away to hit another. A skilled Aborigine could make the weapon literally skip across the ground. Aimed at the legs of large animals, the boomerang could easily bring an animal down by breaking its legs. This device was used to kill large animals, like kangaroos, and if thrown into large flocks of birds or schools of fish could yield a great deal of game in short order.

Other Weapons—the Woomera and Shield

While the basic spear was a vital weapon for the Aborigines, the addition of the *woomera,* or spear thrower, greatly added to the natives' success at hunting. The *woomera* is simply a holder for a spear and acts like an extension of the hunter's arm. By using this device, the Aborigines could throw their spears with greater force for longer distances and with increased accuracy.

The Aborigines living in the southeast part of Australia used a special weapon called the "barbed death spear." According to historian John H. Chambers, this spear "consisted of a row of rough stone fragments sealed with gum . . . into a groove at the spearhead. Because of the angle of the chips, when the [spear]head entered an animal or human being it could not be pulled out and caused a fatal loss of blood."[6]

An Aborigine hunter prepares to throw a "barbed death spear," just one of many weapons used by Aborigines for killing game.

Other Animals in the Aborigine Diet

In many areas of Australia, the Aborigines relied on ducks, swans, and wild turkeys as the mainstay of their diet. Another important bird for the natives was the emu, a large flightless bird that was hunted for its meat and eggs. These birds were often caught in large traps. Sharp sticks were placed in a hole in the ground and afterward covered with dry branches and grass. The emus were then chased across the land until they crossed the hole and fell to their deaths.

The Aborigines also made wide use of the many different kinds of snakes and lizards that lived in the desert regions of the continent. *Goanna,* a large lizard, was a popular source of meat. Thrown directly into the fire, *goanna* is said to taste somewhat like pork.

The Aborigines made wide use of the dingo in their hunting. Dingoes are a type of dog that the Aborigines brought with them to Australia. Yellowish in color, the wild dogs were tamed by the natives and used by them to chase hunting prey. When the Aborigines were forced off their land in later years, the dingoes returned to their wild state.

Unlike the indigenous tribes of North America, the Aborigines did not use the bow and arrow. They did, however, make wide use of shields during defensive combat and also during ceremonies. According to Aboriginal historians, "The narrowest shields were used in hand-to-hand combat while large, broad shields protected the bearer against spears. The largest and most spectacular shields were made by the rainforest peoples of northern Queensland, where they were painted with clan designs and colors."[7]

Medicine from Nature

During their thousands of years as the only human occupants of the Australian continent, the Aborigines gained an incredible storehouse of knowledge about the healing effects of certain plants and animals, many of which are still in use today. Aboriginal elders, both men and women, treated and nursed the sick by using a wide variety of roots, grasses, leaves, and herbs, called "bush medicine" by the European settlers.

The leaves of the corkwood tree, for instance, could be used as a kind of pain reliever or sedative. The drug obtained from these leaves is strong enough, in fact, to stun fish when used on the end of a hook or spear. Scientists have recently discovered that corkwood leaves actually contain the drug atropine, a medication used widely in modern medicine for anesthesia and control of muscle spasms.

The *kardangba* tree, another kind of cork tree, has dark powder on its bark. According to Aboriginal elder Bonnie Tucker, "We use the powder on newborn babies who are sick and have a temperature. The babies sleep and then they wake up well. It's also good . . . against sunburn."[8]

The Aborigines also used a number of different leaves as a kind of "chewing tobacco." These leaves were picked from various bushes and trees and provided pain relief for a variety of ailments. When lumped into a wad and carried behind the ear, the Aborigines found the mixture to have stimulant properties that enabled them to travel long distances without tiring.

The leaves of the soapberry tree could be crushed, mixed with water, and used as a kind of antiseptic or cleansing agent on cuts. The Aborigines also used leeches to draw out blood and cure infections. They believed leeches were particularly effective in the treatment of headaches.

Australia is also home to the world's largest worm, known scientifically as *Megascolides australis*. These giant worms often grow up to twelve feet long and are easily six inches in diameter. According to Bryson, "So substantial are they that one can actually hear them moving through the earth."[9] These worms are warm-blooded and have fifteen separate hearts. The Aborigines have long successfully treated rheumatism—or joint pain—by rubbing the affected body part with the crushed-up remains of the worm.

Whether the Aborigines were looking for food or medicine, they always respected the environment around them. They took only enough to feed their own people and never over hunted or over collected in any one area. The Aborigines, therefore, only stayed in any one area for a short period of time. This practice ensured that there would be food for the next season or for the next group to use the area.

Chapter 2

The Dreamtime

The Aborigines are a deeply spiritual people whose religious rituals are a vital part of their culture and way of life. Everything the Aborigines do, from collecting food to making tools, has a sacred as well as a practical meaning. The Aborigines, explains author Marlo Morgan, "believe everything exists on the planet for a reason. Everything has a purpose."[10]

The land is the foundation of the Aborigines' spiritual life. They believe the land is sacred and that it is there to be honored, preserved, and safeguarded. They believe that the earth does not belong to any one person or tribe but is there for all to enjoy and celebrate. The Aborigines, as a result, have lived for thousands of years in perfect harmony with the earth. "If you look at it their way," says legendary travel writer Bruce Chatwin, "the whole of . . . Australia's a sacred site." The author continues: "To wound the earth is to wound yourself, and if others wound the earth, they are wounding you."[11] Author Robyn Davidson explains the importance of the

land in this way: "[The land] is everything—their law, their ethics, their reason for existence. Without that relationship they become ghosts. Half people. . . . When they lose [the land] they lose themselves, their spirit, their culture."[12]

The Dreamtime

The Aborigines center their entire existence and spiritual life around a mystical concept called the Dreamtime. Their belief in the Dreamtime has little to do with the dreams people of all cultures experience while sleeping. Dreamtime, instead, refers to the beginnings of life and the creation of the world as the Aborigines know it.

The Aborigines believe that before the Dreamtime, Australia was a flat, uninhabited land. Then the Spirit Ancestors, huge semi–human beings and creatures, came up from under the earth and walked across the land singing. Whatever they sang about was created—plants, animals, and human beings. And as they passed on—or as the Dreamtime ended—wherever they had been, the Ancestors turned the land into mountains, hills, valleys, rocks, or waterways. These ancient beings also left behind their spirits to live within the sacred places of the landscape.

In addition to creating the world, the Ancestors left behind all the laws by which the Aborigines were to live their lives. These laws governed the way people lived and how they should behave. They covered social structures, family relationships, and relationships between the people and the natural world. Those who did not follow the rules were punished.

Dr. Irene Watson, an Aboriginal leader, sums up the Aborigines' connection to the land and their belief in the Dreamtime as follows:

The land is sacred because the essence of our spirituality lies in the earth; our spirit guides are resting in the mountains, in the rocks, in the rivers, and they are everywhere in the land. The land is sacred because it carries the footsteps of our spirit ancestors as they walked every part of the country. The ancestors lie sleeping deep in the earth and we are

The Creation Story of the Gagudju Tribe

The Aborigines' spiritual and religious life revolves around their belief in the Dreamtime and the stories that have been passed down through the generations about the beginnings of life itself. Each Aboriginal tribe has its own version of the creation story. The following story about the creation of the world comes from the Gagudju tribe of Australia. It is recounted by author Stanley Breeden in his article "The First Australians."

"Long, long ago, before the Dreamtime, before time could be counted, the world had no shape. It was soft and wobbly. Then at the beginning of the Dreamtime, Warramurrungundji came out of the sea. A female being in human form, she created the land and gave birth to the people and gave them languages. Other creator beings soon followed. Ginga, the giant crocodile, made the rock country. Marrawuti, the sea eagle, brought waterlilies in his claws and planted them on the floodplain. Once the spirit ancestors had completed their creative acts, they put themselves into the landscape, where they remain to this day.

Warramurrungundji, for instance, is a large white rock and Ginga is a rock outcropping textured like the scales on a crocodile's back. These places are called Dreaming Sites and are believed by the Aborigines to still contain the power and energy of the Dreamtime."

responsible for the care of their places . . . for their creative powers are alive.[13]

Dreamtime figures, like the ones depicted in this rock painting, are central elements in the Aborigines' creation stories.

Myths of the Dreamtime

Each Aboriginal tribe has its own Dreamtime stories and myths that explain the land around them. According to mythologist Johanna Lambert, "Dreamtime stories are the predecessors of what we have come to call myths."[14] For some tribes, for example, legions of python snakes slithered from the land in the east, carving out gorges and rivers. Another group of Aborigines has a myth that describes a huge and violent clash between the emu and the turkey. This fight led to the emu losing its wings and forever afterward being unable to fly. Like other people around the world, the Aborigines' myths explain life and the world around them.

For the Aborigines who live in the Northern Territory, the Lightning Man, or Namarrgon, is one of their many mythical beings. According to their legend, the Lightning Man

found his soul mate in a beautiful goddess named *Barrkinj* and the two of them fell hopelessly in love, but then tragedy struck. An evil spirit abducted *Barrkinj* and ever since then Namarrgon has wandered the earth searching for his lost love. He vents his anger with electrical fury, scorching the land with his lightning bolts in an endless quest to flush the evil spirit from his hiding place.[15]

Aboriginal residents use this myth to help explain why their section of the Northern Territory has more lightning strikes than anywhere else in the world.

Songlines and Dream Journeys

The journeys of the Spirit Ancestors across the land are recorded in Dreaming Tracks or Songlines. These tracks are imaginary lines that trace the paths taken by the Ancestors as they moved through the landscape, forming its features and creating its plants and animals. An Aboriginal tribe traditionally described its territory through songs instead of maps. Providing an Aborigine knew the songs, he could always find his way across the country. According to Chatwin, "An unsung land is a dead land, since if the songs are forgotten, the land itself will die. To allow that to happen was the worst of all possible crimes."[16]

The Dream Journey is the name given to the return of an individual to a sacred place of origin each year. Such a journey and each of its stages are filled with incredible significance. To accomplish this task, the Aborigines leave their camps and go on a "walkabout." A walkabout is a journey into the wilderness for ceremonial purposes in order to visit the sacred sites. This sacred trip has often been likened to the pilgrimages taken by Christians and Muslims.

On the Dream Journey, the Aborigines follow the same path their ancestors fol-lowed long ago. This ritual journey has been passed down from one generation to another and has been described as literally "walking in the footprints of the ancestors." The natives carry few possessions with them and instead rely on the land to provide the necessary food as they move from place to place. They sing the ancient songs as they visit those sites that are sacred and important to them, and for which they have been given responsibility.

The Aborigines place tremendous importance on the care of their land. They believe that the Songlines that cross the continent are sacred paths leading into an eternal dimension. According to author Stanley Breeden, "When the ancestral beings had completed their creation, they told the people: 'Now we have done these things, you make sure they remain like this for all time. . . .'"[17] Thus were the Aborigines charged with caring for the land and all living things.

Certain ceremonies must also be performed when visiting a sacred site. Breeden recounts his own experience while visiting the Kakadu area of Australia:

The rock stands at the entrance to a deep canyon of great importance in *Gagudju* [tribe] mythology. As soon as we arrive, *Kapirigi,* a somewhat frail figure with gray hair and long beard, steps onto a prominent boulder, holding a spear. Facing the rock's glowing face, he speaks to the rock and the canyon in a ringing voice, like a messenger from another world.

Ceremonies

Ceremonies are the way that the Aborigines celebrate their spiritual relationship with the land. Each Aboriginal tribe's land has different sites that are spiritually significant. Clans and specific individuals are entrusted with the care and responsibility of these sites. Ceremonies must be held to ensure that the ancestral powers renew the land and all the life contained within it.

Only men participate in these sacred ceremonies. They paint their faces and bodies with ocher. They use white clay to make dots, stripes, and other elaborate patterns, while drawings of lizards, snakes, kangaroos, and other significant animals are drawn with red and yellow ocher. Usually, the tribal elders are the most elaborately painted and attired.

Many elders wear headdresses made out of bright bird feathers, while others don necklaces and other jewelry made out of stones and seeds. Ankle bracelets made of large pods create the sounds of pulsating rattles as seeds bounce around inside the pod. Various tribal members play ancient musical instruments as they sing and chant sacred songs.

Sand paintings are often used as backdrops for Aboriginal religious ceremonies. Blood and water are sometimes used to harden the ground. A sacred painting is then created by utilizing yellow and red ochers, along with feathers and other materials.

In his own language he announces his presence to the spirits there, asking their permission to enter.[18]

Aboriginal women have their own song cycles. They must visit different sacred sites and are responsible for the protection and celebration of these landmarks.

Uluru

Located in the middle of Australia, Uluru is one of the most sacred of all Aboriginal Dreamtime sites. Uluru is a monolith, meaning it is made entirely out of rock, and is estimated to be over 600 million years old. Two miles long, it is over a thousand feet high and can be seen for miles around. The rock is one of Australia's most popular tourist attractions and is famous for its color changes throughout the day as it turns from pink to red to deep purple. For many years the huge rock was called Ayers Rock, but when the site was returned to its Aboriginal "owners" in 1985, the ancient and sacred name of Uluru came into use once again. Uluru means "shadowy place" in the local languages.

According to Aboriginal belief, Uluru is the home of the Sacred Water Python, the benign lizard Kandju, and the hare-wallaby and carpet-snake people. "Every crack, crevice, indentation, lump and striation," writes Jennifer Westwood,

> had a meaning to the local Aborigines. The water stain down one side was the blood of the venomous snake people, conquered in a famous Dreamtime battle. The holes in one boulder were the eyes of a long-dead enemy; the lump on another was the nose of an ancestor now asleep. And each cave around the base of the rock had a purpose in the rituals of the Aborigines.[19]

Uluru has always been the Dreamtime home of the Pitjantjatjara, the hare-wallaby people who live on the north side of the rock, and of the Yankuntjatjara, the carpet-snake people who live on the south side. These two tribes of Aborigines now run many of the tours of the ancient site and explain the ancient stories to visitors from around the world.

Totems

Each Aboriginal person has his or her own totem figure. A totem is an animal, plant, rock, or item of special spiritual significance. Many natives receive this totem at birth or just before they are born. A mother or father might receive a significant sign that their child has a particular totem. For example, a group of wallabies might appear while one of the parents is out walking. This sign may be interpreted to indicate that when the baby is born he or she will be spiritually linked to the wallaby totem. This spiritual link between a child and a totem is referred to as a person's Dreaming.

Every Kangaroo Man, for instance, believes he is descended from a universal Kangaroo Father, who is the ancestor of all other Kangaroo Men and of all living kangaroos. All kangaroos are, therefore, his brothers. He is forbidden from killing such an animal as this act is seen as the same as killing a relative. In that way, the kangaroos would live on as part of the Dreaming.

Each person also has a strong bond to the sacred sites that are associated with his or her totems. Each clan also honors its own totem. Through honoring their totems, the Aborigines are able to keep in touch with nature and the Dreamtime.

Elders and Medicine Men

There are no priests or other clergy in the Aboriginal community. Instead, the Aborigines rely on elders (wise men and women) to communicate with the spirit world. It is the responsibility of the elders to pass on Dreamtime stories and to share spiritual messages with other tribal members.

In the past many elders were also tribal doctors or medicine men, called *karadji*. The work of the *karadji* included curing sickness, predicting the future, and determining the causes of death. The Aborigines believed that medicine men could also make rain and stop it from falling.

More frequently than not, a father would initiate his son into the role of tribal

Two Aborigine elders smoke a ceremonial pipe, which is community property.

doctor or medicine man. "Because of [the *karadji*'s] direct contact with the Dreaming," writes James Cowan, "he was one of the few people able to create new dances, songs and stories. Through him, a tribal community could remain culturally vital and grow accordingly."[20]

In addition, according to Aboriginal belief, the *karadji* had vast "seeing" powers. This meant that the tribal doctors had the ability to see into the future and the past. This ability was used to see what was phys-

ically wrong with a patient and determine whether an illness had been caused by a curse or evil spirit. They accomplished this task by using a wide variety of natural remedies, magic, or through "out-of-body" journeys. According to historian John H. Chambers, "The Aborigines believed that through magic, men could see into the future, walk on the air several feet above the ground, and travel on spirit journeys."[21]

The Aborigines believed that sickness was caused by an evil spirit entering a person's body. According to the Aborigines of the rain forest, for example, only a *dambunji,* or evil sorcerer, could cause an evil spirit to act in this way. The affected person could be cured only by a tribal doctor "removing" the offending spirit. This was done during a special ceremony where the doctor rubbed or sucked on the diseased parts of the body.

It was also commonly believed that death was usually caused by sorcery or magic, rather than any natural causes. Chambers explains, "The Aboriginal mind was so deeply committed to magical beliefs that it was widely believed that sorcerers could kill at a distance by projecting small missiles such as small stones and quartz crystals out of their mouths, and at great velocity, into the bodies of their victims."[22]

Most Aborigines believe that after death they will be reunited with their ancestors. Many also believe that someday the Dreaming will return and give new life to Aboriginal values and customs. The return of the Dreamtime, they believe, will result in a cleansing of the earth and, most important, the return of Aboriginal lands to the natives.

Death and Burial Rituals

Early Aborigines, for instance, practiced cremation—the burning of dead bodies. According to historian Scott Forbes, "This is the earliest evidence of complex death rites found anywhere in the world."[23] When an Aborigine died, it was the responsibility of the entire tribe to

make sure the individual was properly buried. Depending on the part of the country they lived in and the customs followed, each tribe differed somewhat in the methods of burial they used.

Some groups bury their dead wrapped in mummy fashion in tombs that are cut into the sides of mountains. Morgan writes, "The Aborigines don't place much significance in the dead human body, so it is often buried in a shallow grave. . . . Some natives request being left uncovered in the desert so they become food for the animal kingdom."[24]

When a Gagudju Aborigine dies, explains Breeden, "he is wrapped in a sheet of paperbark and then either buried or placed on a platform high in a tree. A year or so later, the bones are recovered, painted . . . red . . . and ceremonially placed in a small cave."[25] These rituals must be done correctly in order to liberate the person's spirit.

The Aborigines who live in the tropical rain forests of Australia keep a tribal burial ground. An ordinary rock is placed on each grave. The size and shape of the rock identifies those who are buried there. At burial services, tribal elders offer prayers and ask the spirit of the deceased to "stay put." These Aborigines believe that after several days the spirit will leave the body and take up "residence" in a rock, a tree, or an animal from which it will then watch over the tribe.

Smoking the Dead

Traditionally, a death among the Kooma and other Aboriginal tribes was followed by a practice called "smoking." This procedure was done about a week after the person died. The ritual was based on the natives' belief that the spirit of the deceased wanted to continue its journey to the afterworld but might be tempted to linger at home because of familiar smells. Many dwellings were simply burned down.

Many Aboriginal women in modern Australia continue this custom by walking through a house where someone has died with a bucketful of burning leaves. The Aborigines believe that the smoke clears away the bad spirits left after a death and also serves to remove personal smells that might linger. Once the "smoking" has been accomplished, according to Aboriginal belief, the spirit of the deceased will be released to continue its journey to the spirit world. During this ritual Aboriginal children are often kept within their houses at night so the spirit of the dead cannot snatch them away.

The Aborigines also go to great lengths to ensure that a dead person's name is never spoken out loud. According to Aboriginal historians, "Mentioning the personal name of someone who has died recently can cause offense, anguish and grief."[26] Lambert explains:

Among the *Euahlayi* tribe, the belief is that a deceased person's spirit emerges from the grave to meet his or her dead relatives who will then help the deceased on the journey to the Realm of the Dead. If the deceased's

Aborigines add wood to the funeral pyre of a deceased family member.

Burial Traditions of the Tiwi and Torres Strait Islanders

Different Aboriginal tribes throughout Australia use different methods of burial. On Melville and Bathurst Islands, the Tiwi tribe carves beautiful poles from trees to honor their dead relatives. These Spirit Poles, or Pukumani, are painted with natural dyes and then implanted upright in the ground. The paintings are of symbolic and mythological figures and also feature aspects and key events of the deceased person's life. Funerals are followed by ceremonial dancing and singing at which time family members walk through the smoke of a fire. This ritual is done to ensure that the relative's spirit makes its way to the Spirit World.

The Torres Strait Islanders, on the other hand, are noted for a unique ceremony known as a "tombstone opening." This ceremony marks the end of the grieving process for a deceased relative. For the Is-

landers, the ceremony comes at the end of a three-year-long burial ritual. The unveiling of the actual tombstone is a time of great celebration that includes long prayers, totemic songs, dancing, and feasting.

Pukumani, or Spirit Poles, of carved and painted wood surround the deceased and, according to the beliefs of the Tiwi tribe, act as a guide to the spirit world.

name is called, however, he or she may be tempted to stay as a despairing, disembodied spirit on earth, thus creating havoc among the living.[27]

The Aborigines' belief system, developed in isolation and nurtured without influence for many centuries, incorpo-

rates practices seldom found in modern cultures. Most historians point out, however, that the native Australians lived a very spiritual life. Their belief in the Dreamtime and their respect for the land and all living things enabled the Aborigines to live in peace and harmony for thousands of years.

Chapter 3

Family and Community Life

Prior to the arrival of the Europeans, there were perhaps as many as seven hundred different tribes of Aborigines living in Australia. Each group had its own dialect or language, its own territory, and its own standards of behavior. Each Aboriginal group, in addition to speaking its own language, could usually also speak and understand those of its neighbors.

The Aborigines lived under a complex system of family and community relationships where every person knew his or her place in society. Extended families were at the core of these kinship systems. As Aboriginal historians explain, "Kinship systems define where a person fits in to the community, binding people together in relationships of sharing and obligation."[28]

Tribal Stucture

The Aborigines had neither established formal governments nor rallied around any kind of single political or tribal chief. Instead, a group of elders in each camp was responsible for making decisions and settling disputes. Many tribes, particularly the larger ones, would never actually come together as a whole, not even at ceremonies.

Aborigines belonged, according to native traditions, to local groups called clans. Based on their ties to a common ancestor—parents or grandparents—these extended families, made up of fifteen to thirty members, were the basic unit of Aboriginal society. Each clan or band "owned" certain lands and conducted its own ceremonial rituals.

A group of bands, all speaking the same language or dialect, formed larger units called tribes. Tribes relied on all of their members to work in a cooperative way in order to take advantage of an area's abundant food sources. In times of drought or other scarcity, tribes shared food and other resources with one another. Tribes were also responsible for the upkeep of certain sacred sites and/or objects.

Each Aboriginal tribe had a well-understood set of behavioral standards and a system for enforcing them. An individual who had a complaint presented the problem to a council made up of elders. The judgments handed down by the council could not be challenged or questioned.

Punishments for wrongdoing might include public scolding or the payment of some kind of debt to the injured individual. These payments usually involved the wrongdoer performing some kind of service. In the event of more extreme viola-tions such as murder, the guilty party was banished from camp. This banishment was, in reality, a death sentence since few could survive in the harsh environment on their own.

Intertribal Relations

The Aborigines were very active traders. Trade routes between different groups of natives crisscrossed Australia. Many Aboriginal groups traveled hundreds of miles to participate in large get-togethers similar to flea markets today.

A council of elders meets to discuss and resolve tribal issues.

Storytelling

Storytelling plays an important role in the everyday life of the Aborigines. Stories are used to pass on knowledge about life; the tribe's heritage, laws, and history; and how the land and people came into being. From an early age, storytelling plays a vital role in the education of Aboriginal children.

This story is recounted by Linda Christmas in her book *The Ribbon and the Ragged Square*. It tells the story of how the koala, a tree-climbing marsupial, came into existence.

"Long ago there was an orphan boy named Koober who was treated very badly by his relatives. He was never given enough water to drink and was only allowed to eat the leaves from the gum or eucalyptus tree. One day, Koober's relatives all left to go looking for food but they forgot to hide their water buckets.

Koober took the buckets and hung them in the branches of a nearby gum tree. He then climbed the tree and chanted a song that made the tree grow bigger and greener. When Koober's relatives returned the tree was bigger than they remembered but not quite high enough to hide the young boy. The relatives climbed the tree and threw the boy to the ground. They watched as the boy's shattered body turned into a koala.

The koala quickly climbed back into the tree. To this day, the animal lives on the leaves of the gum tree and does not need water to keep him alive. (In fact, the koala's Aboriginal name means 'one who doesn't drink.')

And that is how the koala came to live in the eucalyptus or gum tree."

Raw materials such as ocher (colored rocks used for painting and body decoration) and shells along with craft items were popular trading items. In addition, tools, music, art, and stories were also passed from group to group along these trading routes. Goods were sometimes exchanged to settle marriage arrangements, legal agreements, or disputes.

This trade would continue in future years between the Aborigines and the British. The Europeans needed food while the natives wanted European iron and steel tools. But, according to Aboriginal historians, the native people were content to live off the land and, "unlike the natives of other lands, . . . showed no interest in the knick knacks of the European colonists."[29]

Since the Aborigines had few material possessions to fight over and were not inclined to accumulate property or storable wealth, they rarely engaged in organized warfare against neighboring tribes. Historian Russel Ward writes that "they were the least political and warlike peoples known in history."[30]

On the few occasions where tribes did fight one another, it was usually over the rights for the best watering holes or hunting territories. These skirmishes were usually brief and involved small groups of people. In addition, feuds between neighboring clans might also develop over wrongs or violence done to individual clan members. Fights or "duels" usually settled these arguments. The two tribes or clans gathered and watched as the two individuals threw spears at each other or fought in hand-to-hand combat. According to writer Allen L. Johnson, "Once the pair settled the dispute, whatever the outcome, the tribes went peacefully on their ways."[31] In fact, the Aborigines often cemented such settlements with an intertribal marriage.

Marriage

Everyone in Aboriginal society was expected to marry. In most cases, marriages were arranged within the tribe, usually when the children were extremely young. A child's parents, grandparents, or even a favorite uncle took responsibility for making the necessary arrangements. A marriage would not, however, occur until the prospective bride had had her first menstrual period.

Many of the marriages were ones of convenience. Marrying into a strong

family, for instance, or one with strong sorcery skills resulted in increased social standing within the native community. Arranged marriages were also a way to end long-standing feuds between neighboring tribes. Being related by marriage often ended the bloodshed because in Aboriginal society marriage united two families and clans, not just two individuals.

Older men within a clan were usually given the first opportunity when it came time to select marrying partners. A woman who had lost her husband through death was expected to remarry and often ended up marrying one of her husband's relatives. Marriage between cousins was not uncommon, nor was it unusual for a man to be married to more than one wife. Any unhappy or abusive marriage could be dissolved by one of the two parties moving away.

Among the Kuku Yalanji of northern Queensland, girls were "sung" to during the courtship period. According to native practice, a young man could put a "spell" on his promised partner in order to earn her affection. This was done by stealing an article of her clothing or even a piece of her hair and then singing a chant over the item. Occasionally the young man would have a medicine man make a love potion to help woo the girl.

If all went well, the couple would agree to marry. After the proper length of time, as ordained by tribal custom, the girl simply moved in with the man and they were considered married.

Relationships Between Men and Women

According to traditional Aboriginal belief, in the beginning women possessed all the knowledge that existed. As Johnson explains, "The women soon realized this was not right so according to the women they gave part of the knowledge to men. The men's version is that they [the men] stole it."[32] The discrepancy between the two versions seems to have set the stage for poor relation between the

Corroborees

The Aborigines of Australia frequently held large traditional festivals called *corroborees*. These celebrations might be held after a tribe escaped some specific danger like a drought. Or they might occur to honor the guardian spirits of the land or to mark the initiation of young boys into full manhood.

Aboriginal men always took the main role at *corroborees* by painting their bodies and dancing. The several days–long festival often included sporting contests where men challenged one another to see who could throw a spear or boomerang the farthest. Most of the music at these celebrations came from the traditional instrument of the Aborigines—the didgeridoo.

Aboriginal women usually played a secondary role at *corroborees*. They traditionally prepared the food but attended the dances and music performances as spectators, not participants. Female Aborigines also held their own festivities to mark the entrance to puberty of young women.

Corroborees, which are still held in Australia, are community events, and now every member of the clan is expected to participate. Children learn dance and song at an early age and are encouraged to join in the festivities.

Aboriginal men dance to the music of the didgeridoo at a corroboree, *a traditional Aborigine festival.*

An Aborigine woman shares in the labor of the tribe by weaving a basket.

sexes at least in certain Aboriginal societies. For in some groups, according to historian John H. Chambers, "men brutalized their women. There are well-documented accounts, from every part of the continent, of Aboriginal women being beaten with clubs, dragged around the campsite. . . ."[33]

Other historians disagree and report that women held a very strong position in Aboriginal society and were much respected. While native men and women had separate roles, their roles were actually part of a single function aimed at survival. Men and women cooperated in hunting and food gathering. The men were responsible for the hunting and for making stone tools. Women, on the other hand, gathered food and were responsible for the making of baskets and such minimal clothing as the Aborigines wore.

Relationship and Marriage Rules

"Social relations," explains Chambers, "allowed for the ceremonial exchange of women and the sexual favors of women were commonly bestowed as a gesture of friendship."[34] This swapping of wives was considered a sign of brotherhood. Historian Robert Hughes writes: "As a mark of hospitality, wives were lent to [those] visitors the . . . tribesmen wanted to honor."[35]

Like many other indigenous peoples, the Aborigines had certain rules about marriage and relationships that needed to be followed. In many native communities, relatives were required to keep a certain physical distance between themselves and members of their immediate family, other than children. If a man saw his mother-in-law coming down a path toward him, for instance, he was forbidden to speak to her. In addition, he was required by traditional "law" to step aside and allow her to pass. Touching one another was also deeply frowned upon. "Even today," writes Chambers, "in tribes such as the *Tiwi,* once past puberty, brothers and sisters are forbidden to even speak to one another."[36]

Children

Because of their nomadic way of life, the Aborigines did not want large families. In order to keep their families small, many tribes practiced a form of induced abortion using herbal medicine. In some areas of Australia, men also refrained from having sex with their wives during the extended breast-feeding phase. Children were fed on breast milk until they were at least three years old. This was essential as there were no goats or cows to use for milk.

Many Aborigines used smoke in a ritual following the birth of a child. Called "smoking the baby," the natives believed this practice of fanning smoke over a newborn would give the child a healthy start in life.

Each Aboriginal child is named at birth. It is understood, however, that throughout each person's lifetime, the birth name could be changed. Each individual is allowed to select a new name that is based on their roles within a given community. Marlo Morgan, during her trip through the Outback with a tribe of Aborigines, reported: "Our group contained Story Teller, Tool Maker, Secret Keeper, Sewing Master, and Big Music, among others."[37]

Aboriginal children were not just the concern of the biological parents but of the entire community. As a result, the raising, care, education, and discipline of children were the responsibility of all tribal members. This practice of community upbringing continues today. Said Wadjularbinna Doomadgee, a member of the Gungalidda tribe, in 1996: "All people with the same skin grouping as my mother are my mothers. . . . They have the right, the same as my mother, to watch over, to control what I'm doing, to make sure that I do the right thing. It's an extended family thing."[38]

Games

Aboriginal children played games with toy digging sticks and spears and learned early on hunting and gathering skills they would

Music

The Aborigines are a very musical people. In addition to learning the songs of their Dreaming Tracks, the natives also use a wide variety of musical instruments. These instruments are played at *corroborees,* other celebrations, and in the evening when the tribe gathers around the campfire.

The instrument most frequently associated with the Aborigines is the didgeridoo (sometimes spelled *didjeridu*). The word "didgeridoo" is an Aboriginal term that means "drone pipe." Made from a single length of hollow bamboo or other tree branch, the instrument produces a sound that has been described as similar to a foghorn. It is a haunting sound. High squeals combine with deep growling noises to produce incredible music.

In addition to the didgeridoo, the Aborigines also utilize a number of other musical instruments. These can be very simple, like the clapping of hands, or more complicated, such as the instrument called the *kulup*. The *kulup* is a hand shaker filled with seeds. It is made of wood that has been tied together with special twine. When shaken it makes a sound similar to that of Native American rattles.

Gong stones are used by some tribes. These "musical stones" are obtained from sacred caves and come in different sizes and shapes. Different sounds are made by hitting the stones together. Clap sticks are also a favorite instrument. Also called "message sticks," they are made from hardwood. As they are hit together, they produce different musical notes.

An Aborigine man plays the didgeridoo.

need later in life. Those who lived along the coasts of Australia used coconuts to play various kinds of ball games.

A favorite children's game was cat's cradle, a game that has been played by Native American children as well. A piece of string or twine is looped over the fingers of both hands. By moving the fingers and the string, a number of shapes can be created. A lizard, crocodile, lightning bolt, canoe, and crab are just a few of the shapes that can be formed.

Hundreds of years before the white race took up the sport, Australian Aborigines invented and played football. This game is not the same as the football played all over North America, but rather more like soccer. "Football is part of our culture," writes Aborigine Michael Long. "Tribes came together to compete in hunting, fishing, running, spear throwing and also football—kicking a ball, often made of an animal skin filled with mud or animal dung. . . . The football game was seen as a show of strength, that one tribe was stronger than the other, but it was also played for fun."[39] The game was usually played naked prior to the arrival of the Europeans.

Initiation into Manhood

Each tribe or clan used special rituals and ceremonies to prepare boys for becoming adults. These rites were different from group to group, but all included tests of strength and endurance, ceremonial painting, dancing, and singing. Initiation also involved the passing down of religious and cultural knowledge. The ritual prac-

tices that marked the passage from girlhood to womanhood were less elaborate.

In various parts of Australia, young Aborigines also underwent certain painful physical procedures. According to historian Chambers, "In Central Australia, the *Aranda* people tore out the initiate's fingernails. In the Canberra area, elders singed off all the hair from an initiate's head. Circumcision was almost universally practiced. . . . These things were [all] aimed at spiritual release."[40]

In Arnhem Land, as late as the 1920s, candidates for manhood underwent a two-week-long series of trials. "The third test," writes historian Roff Smith, "demanded that they bake in the sun for a full day without food or water."[41] Once the physical tasks had been completed, the boy was sent into the wilderness. For the young men of the Walleroo tribe, the last stage in the initiation was a long crawl through a sacred cave. When the boy emerged, he was considered a man and was told the sacred stories and songs of the people. Once he returned to camp, the tribal members were required to treat him with respect.

A great and exciting celebratory dance was then held, sponsored by the elders and men of the tribe. Each new initiate was required to perform a special dance given to him in visions or dreams that had come to him while in the wilderness. Each man elaborately decorated his body with ashes, feathers, and various colors of paint. The dancing, singing, and feasting might go on for days.

The Rock Art Tradition

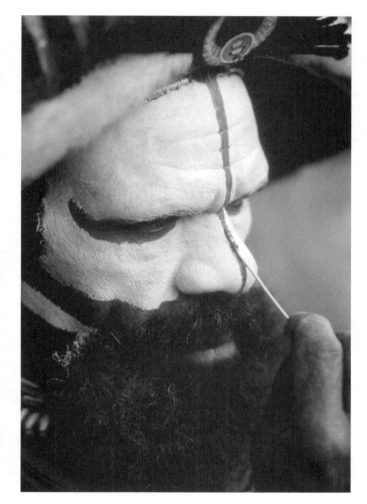

An Aborigine man paints his face in preparation for a ceremony.

In the many thousands of years that they have occupied Australia, the Aborigines have created some of the most beautiful and compelling art galleries in the world. These galleries, found in caves and rocks throughout the continent, contain magnificent drawings and engravings. Some of this rock art dates back over fifty thousand years.

With no written language, rock art has been the Aborigines' way of recording their history. The paintings honor the land, depicted Dreamtime stories, and were an ingenious way to pass on their creation stories and history to future generations. In describing this rock art, author Tim Cahill writes: "There was a history there . . . the record of a culture, a record that encompassed countless cultures."[42] The paintings reveal how the Aborigines saw themselves, their world, and their place in it.

Archaeologists have been able to gain a very accurate pictorial history of Australia by looking at the Aborigines' rock art sites. The arrival of the Europeans was recorded in paintings of sailing ships and helmeted figures with pipes. Rock

One of the final and most important parts of the initiation rites was the disclosure of the location of places, such as caves and mountains, that were sacred to the tribe. The young men were often taken to these sacred sites, where they were shown vast art galleries depicting the tribe's history.

Ocher

For centuries Aborigines have used ocher to make paint. Ocher is a colored rock that when crushed into a fine powder and mixed with water, makes various colors of paint. Ocher has also been used as medicine and as a valuable trading item with other tribes. Red ocher, for instance, when mixed with grease and eucalyptus leaves, combines to form a decongestant that helps in the treatment of colds.

Aborigines also used black paint. This was usually made from crushed charcoal, while white paint was obtained from pipe clay. The natives widely believed that white ocher had magical powers. According to traditional beliefs, when white ocher was mixed with water and blown from the mouth, the result was calm winds and cooler days. Paint could also be made from different-colored clays, vegetable dyes, and blood.

In addition to rock art painting, the various shades of ocher and paint were also used for body decorations and for making designs on weapons and other implements. Brushes for painting were generally made by crushing the end of a green stick and using the crushed end as bristles. To do fine drawing, the Aborigines utilized a small twig or a stalk of strong grass.

art also shows changes in Aboriginal tools as well as the climate changes that affected the continent. A rock mural in the Northern Territory illustrates what historians believe to be one of the world's earliest battle scenes. It depicts over a hundred stick figures charging one another and throwing spears.

The Aborigines believe that it is important for the survival of their cultures to renew these paintings periodically. Only certain Aboriginal elders and medicine men are allowed to do this restoring and repainting. By maintaining the ancient sacred sites, people today are attempting to keep the Dreamtime alive for all the tribes.

Kinds of Rock Art

Archaeologists and art historians have identified several distinct styles of rock art painting. One of the earliest known forms of painting is known as the "naturalist" style. These paintings depict animals and clearly demonstrate the importance of certain species in Aboriginal society. In the northeast, along the Cape York Peninsula, for instance, dugongs, once a valuable source of food for the coastal natives, swim across the walls of caves along with giant crocodiles and turtles. In other areas of Australia, kangaroos, emus, fish, and wallabies dot rock formations. According to author Stanley Breeden, "The act of painting, together with certain rituals, ensures that the animals will always be available, both as food and for the people's Dreaming."[43]

One of the most unusual styles of rock art is called "X-ray painting." Found mainly in the western part of Arnhem Land, these drawings show not only the bodies of people and animals, but their skeletons and internal organs as well.

One of the most popular themes of rock art is the presentation of various supernat-ural figures. Some of the spookiest images thus far discovered are those of the Quinkans. These large, thin, and sinister figures with staring eyes are apparently malicious supernatural spirits who dwell in cracks in large rocks. Even more inter-esting are the Wandjinas. Found in the Kimberley area of Australia, Wandjinas are ancestral beings from the sea and sky. According to Aboriginal belief, these spir-its formed the landscape and were respon-sible for creating lightning, storms, and great floods.

This Aboriginal painting depicting characters from a creation myth typifies the "X-ray" style of rock art found mainly in the western part of Arnhem Land.

Bark Painting and Basketry

Bark paintings were first used as decorations for the interiors of Aboriginal shelters along the seacoast. A typical painting, for instance, might tell the story of a hunting trip or an expedition to collect seagull eggs.

The stringybark tree, a kind of gum tree, is one source of the bark used in making these paintings. Another is the messmate tree of northern Queensland. In both cases, the bark is cut from the living tree during the wet season at a time when the sap is flowing freely. The sap's presence allows the bark to come away cleanly and easily from the tree. The bark is then straightened by placing it over an open fire. It does not burn because of the moisture still contained within it. Once the bark has been dried, it makes a wonderful medium for painting. This style of art is still widely practiced throughout Australia today.

Aboriginal women were responsible for making the baskets and other containers used in food gathering. Many of the baskets and bags were woven from bark, while others contained human hair, palm fronds, and grasses. Bush twine was used to hold them together, and they were often colored with dyes made from roots and other natural substances. Aboriginal baskets were frequently decorated with feathers, shells, and other objects.

The Wandjinas are huge figures that have been painted white. They have black eyes and noses, but no mouths. They also have halos of lines radiating out from their heads. These halos are believed to represent lightning. The Aborigines believe these figures can retain their magic for centuries. Only a few select Aboriginal elders are allowed to repaint them so as to renew the figures' spiritual qualities.

Isolated on the continent of Australia, the Aborigines, over many thousands of years, developed a rich and unique society and culture. Their way of life, however, was soon to be shaken to its very core.

Chapter 4

A Clash of Cultures

For centuries the Aborigines believed they were the only people on earth. Unknown to them, thousands of miles away, Europeans had long wondered about the possible existence of a southern continent. In the second century, ancient Greek geographer Ptolemy wrote about such a land, believing that the weight of such a continent was necessary in order to balance the globe. Ptolemy called this unknown land *Terra Australis Incognita,* a Latin phrase meaning "unknown southern land."

The Macassans

It was not the Europeans, however, who were the first to visit this southern continent. That distinction goes to fishermen from Macassar on the Indonesian island of Sulawesi, who, in the early sixteenth century, landed in Australia. The Macassans set up seasonal camps to collect and process an Asian delicacy called trepang. Trepang is a kind of sea cucumber that is very popular in China, where it is still used in soups.

The Macassans also traded goods with coastal Aborigines. Some of the Aborigines may have accompanied the Macassans back to Indonesia, returning to Australia with tales of the things they saw. According to Aboriginal historians, "The Macassan influence can be seen today by loanwords incorporated into . . . languages, [and] in rock paintings."[44] The rock paintings, done by the Aborigines, depict the arrival of the Macassans and the interactions between the two groups.

First Sightings

The honor of the first recorded sighting of Australia goes to the Dutch. In 1606 Willem Jansz landed on the western shore of Cape York Peninsula. Hoping to find riches, he found instead, what historian Roff Smith calls, "shimmering, heat-warped horizons, a parched coast and wild, cruel, black savages."[45] Jansz left Australia a few days later after losing several of his men in fights with the Aborigines.

Tasmania

In 1642 Dutchman Abel Tasman discovered the island of Tasmania, lying south of the continent of Australia. Finding the land inhospitable and the natives hostile to their presence, Tasman and the Dutch were forced to abandon any hopes of settling the land. The English would soon "rediscover" the island and move in.

Originally part of the same landmass, Tasmania separated from the mainland of Australia about thirteen thousand years ago, isolating both the natives and the animals on the two islands. Thereafter, the Aborigines on Tasmania developed new ways of life and began to look slightly different from the natives of Australia.

While on the mainland people developed such specialized hunting tools as boomerangs and *woomeras,* the Tasmanians used simpler tools and plain wooden spears. Unlike their cousins on the mainland, the Tasmanians developed boat designs and built canoes made out of rolls of bark that were capable of carrying entire families.

According to historians, the Aborigines of Tasmania were startling in appearance. The men wore their hair in long ringlets that were smeared with grease and red ocher, while the women kept their heads closely shaved. To keep out the cold, the natives coated their bodies with a mixture of animal fat, ocher, and charcoal. This covering was also fairly successful in keeping away the hordes of insects that flourished on the island.

The natives thrived on their island home until the early 1800s when the first British settlers arrived and totally disrupted their way of life.

The next explorer to land on the shores of Australia was another Dutchman, Jan Carstensz, in 1623. The Dutch sent a landing party ashore, where they were met by a large group of the natives. The sailors seized an Aborigine and forcibly took him back to the ship. A near riot broke out on the beach, and the next morning Aborigines attacked a group of sailors sent ashore to chop wood. The Dutch fired several shots, killing one native. The others quickly fled. Carstensz,

finding the land inhospitable, soon sailed away.

English explorer William Dampier arrived in Australia in 1688. At that time Great Britain was hoping to find land in the South Pacific to use as a stopover for English ships. Dampier, however, reported that the land was barren and dry and that the natives had the "most unpleasant looks of any people that I ever met."[46] Dampier sailed away from Australia, leaving the continent untouched for almost another one hundred years.

Historians don't know what the Aborigines thought of these early newcomers. Native rock art, however, clearly depicts the foreigners' arrival in the form of sailing ships and white figures with helmets.

Captain James Cook

In 1768 noted explorer James Cook of England, aboard his ship the *Endeavour*, set sail on an expedition to explore the South Pacific. After spending six months charting the coast of nearby New Zealand, Cook headed south toward Australia. On April 28, 1770, Cook and his crew sighted land, and the following day the *Endeavour* entered a large bay and dropped anchor in what he named Botany Bay—present-day Sydney Harbor. The name "Botany" was used because of the discovery of so many new species of plants and trees.

During the next few weeks, Cook sailed up the coast of Australia and claimed the entire eastern half of the continent in the name of King George III of England. Despite his recorded observation that native people were occupying the land, Cook called the land New South Wales and declared it *"terra nullius,"* or "no-man's-land." Asserting that the continent belonged to no one, Cook claimed it for Great Britain. According to Aboriginal sources, what Cook proba-

Captain James Cook claimed the eastern half of the Australian continent for the English king when he landed there in 1770.

bly meant was that "the human beings of the continent were not like his kind [that is, not white] . . . and were thus aborigines or even sub-human and, therefore, this land was empty."[47] And free for the taking.

Cook went on to report the first recorded words ever spoken by an Aborigine. According to Cook, when the natives sighted the white men, they yelled, *"Warra, Warra!"*—or "Go away." Cook wrote: "All they seem'd to want was for us to be gone."[48]

The First Fleet

Despite Captain Cook's landing in Australia and the reports he sent back to England, Australia might have been left alone for another hundred years had it not been for events occurring elsewhere in the British Empire. On July 4, 1776, the English colonies in America declared their independence.

As war waged in America, the British realized that they could no longer use the colonies of Virginia, Georgia, and the Carolinas as places to send convicts. With a backlog of convicts building up, Great Britain turned south to the continent of Australia.

In January 1788 a flotilla of eleven ships, called the First Fleet, arrived in Botany Bay under the command of Captain Arthur Phillip. On board the vessels were nearly 800 convicts (men, women, and children), along with 250 soldiers and administrators. Phillip became, at that time, the first governor of New South Wales.

As Captain Phillip's colonists landed, a group of Aborigines watched from shore. No one asked their permission, and no one ever negotiated with them about settling on the land. In the beginning the Aborigines were friendly and might have even thought that the newcomers were the spirits of their ancient ancestors. In addition, according to writer Linda Christmas, "they [also] thought . . . that the white man wouldn't stay. Others had come and gone. Such was their early confidence, they felt that even if he did stay, he might well adapt to their way of life, or at least be prepared to share the vast land."[49]

A Clash of Cultures

"Nowhere else in the whole history of the world," writes historian John H. Chambers,

> has there been a greater difference in two civilizations at first contact. The late 18th century Aborigines had an Old Stone Age culture [originating about 2 million years ago], while the British settlers were citizens of what was at the time the world's first and only industrialized society. . . . A people whose tribes held land communally now encountered a people for whom private property was sacrosanct. People, who lacking pottery and metal objects . . . were now face to face with people who had harnessed the mighty powers of iron and steam. . . . This was like an encounter between the inhabitants of different planets. It was inevitable that race relations would be characterized by . . . misunderstanding, tension and tragedy.[50]

Within a few short years, according to Smith, "ancient traditions and cultures built over fifty thousand years crumbled and vanished."[51] From communities that for thousands of years had lived in harmony with one another and the earth, the Aborigines became a people threatened with destruction and extinction.

Pemulwuy

A native named Pemulwuy was perhaps the first Aboriginal guerrilla fighter. In 1790, only two years after the colonists' arrival in Australia, he united some of the local tribes in New South Wales and launched a fairly effective campaign against the British. Over the next twelve years, Pemulwuy and his men attacked British settlers and destroyed their crops and livestock. According to Aboriginal legends, Pemulwuy was considered unable to be killed by bullets. He had sustained serious gunshot wounds on two occasions but each time had survived to continue his fighting.

The British ultimately offered a reward for Pemulwuy's capture or death. He was finally killed in a police ambush in 1802, and his head was sent to England as a scientific specimen. Pemulwuy's son Tedbury continued the resistance movement for a few more years. In 1805 Tedbury was captured, and with his arrest, the alliance of tribes broke up and native resistance ended in the New South Wales area.

Entire populations of Aborigines were wiped out by European diseases for which the natives had no immunity. Malaria, smallpox, measles, and influenza swept through the native population. "To show the effects of disease on the Aboriginal population," writes Sarina Singh, "consider that there were an estimated 1500 Yura people living in Sydney at the point of invasion in 1788. By the end of 1789, it is believed that only two Yura had survived the smallpox epidemic."[52] Deaths from European diseases would ultimately kill more Aborigines than all the conflict and warfare combined.

Governor Arthur Phillip's instructions from the British government had been clear. He was "to open an intercourse with the natives, and to conciliate their affec-tions, enjoining all subjects to live in amity and kindness with them."[53] Despite these lofty words, Phillip was totally unable to prevent the hostilities that began to break out between the two groups in the first few years after settlement.

The British Push Onward

With no thought for the Aborigines, the British pushed onward into the continent. "Restless for land and fortune, gold and beef, wool for the textile mills, and coal to fire factory furnaces," Smith writes, "the British shunted aside the original inhabitants and quickly took possession of the land."[54]

As the convicts and other settlers began to move across Australia, they imported cattle and sheep. The best land for raising these animals was the same land

The introduction of cattle ranching to Australia by European settlers destroyed much of the native environment, resulting in starvation for many Aborigines.

the Aborigines used for hunting. Turning the land into farms destroyed the habitats for the animals the Aborigines had relied on for food in the past. Sheep and cattle quickly destroyed ancient water holes and turned grassland into semidesert.

Little thought was given to the wishes or feelings of the Aborigines. Historian Robert Hughes writes that "the destruction of the Australian [Aborigine] was rationalized as natural law [or survival of the fittest]."[55] To the white settlers, the Aborigines were primitive people who had built no towns or cities, knew nothing of Western civilization, and went around naked.

Fences soon dotted the land and blocked ancient routes the Aborigines followed. Familiar plants died out, causing starvation among the original inhabitants of Australia. Starvation led the natives to kill the settlers' sheep and cattle. Whereas the whites took Aboriginal food just as they pleased, the Aborigines were not allowed to kill the settlers' cattle and sheep. Competition for food and water ultimately led to warfare.

Murder and Massacre

Mistreatment and murder of the Aborigines were all too common in Australia throughout the nineteenth century. This behavior, for the most part, was sanctioned by the governments of the various colonies and territories. In 1821, for example, authorities in the Hawkesbury region of New South Wales authorized soldiers "to shoot any group of Aborigines greater than six in number, even if unarmed and entirely innocent of purpose, even if the number included women and children,"[56] according to author Bill Bryson.

These actions were justified with many rationalizations that would not be acceptable to today's Western society. One unidentified British colonist noted: "It will be a happy day for Australia when the natives and kangaroo disappear."[57] Another wrote: "Nothing can stay the dying away of the Aboriginal race which [God] has only allowed to hold the land until replaced by a finer race." And another unnamed observer had this to say about the killing of Aborigines: "There was nothing wrong in it. . . . [I]t was preposterous to suppose they had souls."[58]

In the climate of such unabashedly racist pronouncements, thousands of Aborigines were massacred all over the continent. In

Jandamarra

In the late 1890s, guerrilla fighter Jandamarra led a group of Aborigines in the Kimberley region of Western Australia. He had grown up during a period when the region was being overrun by sheep and cattle ranches. At the age of fourteen, Jandamarra ran away and began his life as an outlaw by shooting livestock. Captured in 1889, he served a brief prison sentence and then, following his release, served as a tracker for the local police.

Upset by the violence being done to his Bunuba tribe, Jandamarra shot a policeman. He fled to the hills, where he and a small group began an intensive series of raids and killings, virtually stopping further white settlement for a brief period of time. According to Aboriginal historians, Jandamarra loved to track down those who were tracking him. He would stand high above them, waving his spear and rifle in the air, taunting them to come and get him.

Toward the end of 1894, the Kimberley government gathered a large group of policemen to pursue the outlaw. The posse met up with the guerrillas in a high cave, where a day-long fight broke out. Despite being wounded, Jandamarra escaped and lived to fight for another three years. He was finally tracked down and killed by another Aborigine in 1897. According to Bunuba elders, Jandamarra's spirit still lives out in the wilderness, near Tunnel Creek, where he was killed.

Queensland alone, for instance, it is estimated that ten thousand Aborigines were killed by settlers and other white citizens. By the end of the nineteenth century, C. J. Dashwood, the Northern Territory's foremost judge, declared to a South Australian Royal Commission that "Aboriginal people were being shot down like crows."[59]

Not only were thousands of natives killed by whites with guns, but thousands of others were killed by other means. According to the Aborigines, "Many of our people were killed by poisoning [our] waterholes and by gifts of poisoned bread left as bait inside . . . huts."[60] These foods, often laced with arsenic and strychnine, resulted in the deaths of entire tribes.

Aboriginal Resistance

Many Aborigines responded to the violence by fighting and resisting. The natives sometimes set fire to the land in an effort to force the settlers and their animals to leave. Others engaged in guerrilla warfare. These small bands of natives fought fiercely. "A pattern of tenacious and often well-organized resistance, ranging from massed frontal attacks through guerrilla warfare to carefully plotted tracking and revenge-murder of individual Europeans for known crimes against tribespeople took place,"[61] writes historian Hughes.

The Aborigines made sneak attacks on small groups of settlers and then disappeared back into the bush. This resistance was so strong in some areas that it delayed the settlement of those territories for several years. The Aborigines, however, were hopelessly outnumbered, and their simple weapons were easily surpassed by the guns of the Europeans. "Bullets, swords and horses were the frontline weapons use [by the Europeans]," writes an unidentified Aboriginal historian. "Using these was like using a hammer to break an egg."[62] The Aborigines fought back bravely with their spears and boomerangs, but there was little chance of the natives stopping the takeover of their land.

Myall Creek

In the many conflicts and clashes between the Aborigines and the Europeans, the whites were seldom held accountable for their actions. A notable exception occurred in 1838 following the massacre of a large group of Aborigines at Myall Creek in New South Wales. In response to the killing of livestock by hungry natives, a group of twelve white settlers attacked a peaceful camp of twenty-eight Aborigines. According to Bryson, "Their captors tied them together . . . men, women and children [and] led them around the countryside for some hours and then abruptly and mercilessly slaughtered them with rifles and swords."[63]

Soon afterward the twelve white men were brought to trial. George Anderson, a white convict servant, testified in court against the accused settlers. Despite testimony in English that an adult had witnessed the settlers massacring the Aborigines without any proof of their wrongdoing, it took a white jury only fifteen minutes to declare all twelve men innocent of any crime.

Several months later, however, after an outcry from the colonial government, seven of the twelve men were brought to trial for a second time. The accused men loudly protested their innocence, going so far as to claim that they hadn't realized killing Aborigines was illegal. At the retrial the seven Europeans were found guilty and later hanged, the first time whites had ever been convicted of the murder of an Aborigine. The ruling did little to discourage the slaughter of the natives, however.

Attempts to Eradicate the Aborigines in Tasmania

At the time of the European settlement of the island of Tasmania in 1803, the Aboriginal population there numbered around five thousand people. The Aborigines' early distrust of these newcomers quickly turned to resistance and hostility when they realized that the British had come to seize their land, not share it. Vicious warfare broke out between the two groups. What followed was, as historian Margo Daly writes,

Other Massacres

In late 1837 and early 1838, Major James Nunn of the New South Wales Mounted Police led an expedition to end the attacks made by local Aborigines on white settlers. Nunn and his men traveled widely throughout the area and eventually cornered a group of Aborigines at Waterloo Creek. According to Aboriginal historians, in a battle lasting only ten minutes, Nunn and his men massacred between forty and fifty innocent people. Nunn's party then continued its mission for the next several days, reportedly killing every Aboriginal person it encountered.

The last large-scale massacres occurred in 1927 in the Kimberley district of Australia and in 1928 in central Australia and the Northern Territory. In all incidents, the killings were done by the police or with their knowledge. In the Kimberley case, local Aborigines had killed a white man. The police and others caught, chained together, and then murdered eleven Aborigines, burning their bodies afterward in their campfire.

In the Northern Territory in 1928, in an action called the Conniston Massacre, Europeans shot and killed over thirty Aborigines after a supposed native attack on a trapper and station owner. A court of inquiry following the incident ruled that the whites had been fully justified to act as they had. Aborigines who wanted to contest this decision were denied legal representation by the federal government.

"one of the most tragic episodes in modern history."[64]

Merchant John Sherwin of Hobart voiced a view held by the majority of white settlers in Tasmania. "They [the Aborigines] must be captured or exterminated."[65]

Tasmanian Aborigines throw spears at a pair of English surveyors. Aborigines responded to the invasion and eventual usurpation of their land with resistence and hostility.

The British colonial government also supported this view and planned their ensuing actions with the goal of ridding the island of all Aborigines. In 1828 Lieutenant Governor George Arthur proclaimed a state of martial law and gave soldiers the order to "shoot on sight." Two years later the government formed the infamous Black Line, an expedition, according to writer David Quammen, "to sweep the Tasmanian Aborigines off the map."[66]

A human line, made up of more than three thousand armed soldiers, convicts, and colonists swept the island over a period of three weeks. Shoulder to shoulder, they thrashed through the woods and meadows searching for Aborigines. According to Singh, "The Black Line was [in reality] a farce; the Aborigines heard the settlers and soldiers coming from miles away."[67] Only one native man and boy were captured; two others were killed. The remainder of the Aborigines escaped.

Removal of the Tasmanian Aborigines

Despite the failure of the Black Line, by the 1830s only an estimated three hundred Aborigines remained on Tasmania. Hundreds had died as a result of poisoned food, and hundreds more had perished from illnesses for which they had no immunity.

Body Snatchers

The discovery of a unique indigenous group of natives in Australia led to a strange and bizarre practice during the nineteenth century. Museums in many European countries wanted to display skeletons and skulls from native people from around the world. There was a great deal of curiosity among scientists about the different races, and museum and government officials were willing to pay big sums of money for "specimens" to study.

The Aborigines, like natives elsewhere, became victims of what historians call "body snatching." Large numbers of native corpses and skeletons were sold to the highest bidder. One of the best-documented cases of this appalling practice involved a young man named William Lanney, who at the time was widely believed to be the last Tasmanian male. When he died in 1869 at the age of thirty-four, his body was sent to Colonial Hospital Morgue in Hobart.

A prominent surgeon named W. L. Crowther sneaked into the morgue shortly after Lanney's death and cut off the man's head. Another surgeon, Dr. George Stokell, cut off the hands and feet and kept enough of the skin to have a tobacco pouch made for himself. None of these acts was considered criminal behavior, and all of them were tacitly endorsed by the doctors' colleagues.

Another case of body snatching involved the corpse of Truganini, the "last" full-blooded Tasmanian woman. Following her death, her body was buried, but in 1878 she was dug up and her bones were sent to the Tasmanian Museum of Art. The museum reconstructed her skeleton and hung it in a glass case for all to see. After much protest, her remains were returned to her people in the late 1970s and laid to rest in the woman's homeland.

Determined to remove even these few natives, the government forced the Aborigines to relocate to Flinders Island, a bleak piece of land off the northeast coast. Many natives died in transit, while others starved to death on the island. Within a few years, their numbers had fallen to less than fifty.

In the late 1840s the Aborigines were moved once again, this time to an old convict station near Hobart called Oyster Cove. The station was in ruins and conditions were deplorable. By 1859 just fourteen Aborigines were still alive. The "last" Tasmanian Aborigine reportedly died in March 1869. In less than seventy-five years of European contact, the Aborigines of Tasmania were believed to be extinct. According to most historians, this killing of an entire population was a clear example of genocide.

The Tasmanian Aborigines might well have disappeared forever had it not been for the abduction and rape of native women by the colonists. Many of these women later gave birth to children who were at least partly Aboriginal. These single-parent families continued to live in traditional ways in isolated areas of Tasmania. Eventually, they gathered together on Cape Barren Island, a small parcel of land the Europeans didn't want.

In 1912 the Tasmanian government deeded these Aborigines the rights to that island. The group continued to increase in size. The land, however, was taken away from them in 1951, when white interests expressed a desire to mine the area. This small group of Aboriginal descendants and others like them are still waging a struggle for land rights and recognition in Australia at the start of the twenty-first century.

Chapter 5

A White Australia

For over a hundred years, the primary goal of the British government—and later, the Australian government—was to rid the continent of the black population. Seeing the Aborigines as primitive and backward, the government did not attempt to find a place for them in the society established by white Europeans and their descendants. The majority of the nineteenth century was spent trying to achieve the goal of making Australia an all-white nation.

While Aboriginal numbers greatly declined during this period of time, the natives proved to be markedly resilient. Without completely abandoning the hope that the Aboriginal race would eventually die out, the government, in the early twentieth century, moved on to a secondary goal—that of controlling and "civilizing" the natives. The first step was to simply round up the Aborigines and force them to live on specified reserves.

Government Reserves

The colonial government of Australia set up Aboriginal reserves on land that the white settlers didn't particularly want. According to writer Robyn Davidson, "Because everyone believed that the indigenous people would eventually die out, allowing them to keep small sections of their land was seen as a temporary measure that would make life easier for the settlers. The blacks were rounded up like cattle by police and citizens on horseback, wielding guns."[68]

One of the first things that was done after the roundups was to require the Aborigines to wear clothing. As James Cowan writes: "The very fact that nomadic Australians did not wear clothes worked against them in the estimation of Europeans. They were regarded as little more than animals."[69]

On these reserves the Aborigines were forced to settle down and become farmers. They were ordered to stop performing their elaborate ceremonies and were forbidden to take their annual pilgrimages to sacred sites. On many of the reserves run by missionaries, the natives were forced to attend church and become Christians. Another practice was to stop the Aboriginal people from speaking their own languages. Because a number of tribes were unable to pass their dialects to future generations, many of the Aboriginal languages were lost forever.

Many Aboriginal men were sent to work on huge sheep and cattle ranches, called stations in Australia. According to historian Roff Smith, "By the turn of the [twentieth] century, the Aborigines had earned renown as the finest riders and wranglers on the range despite never having seen horses or cattle until the arrival of the Europeans."[70] Most of these Aborigines, however, were ill treated and were paid in tobacco and food rather than cash.

Life on the Reserves

For many thousands of years, the Aborigines had been a nomadic people, moving from place to place with the seasons. By the beginning of the twentieth century, the majority of natives were living on reserves, where they were treated like prisoners and forbidden to leave the compounds. Many of these reserves would continue to operate well into even the late twentieth century. Until the 1980s Aborig-

Aborigines wearing European-style clothing pose with foreign settlers.

The Gold Rush

For the first fifty-plus years of its existence as a British colony, Australia served primarily as a prison for English convicts. Gradually, however, over time the number of free citizens began to overtake those of the prisoners. A major factor in eventually making Australia a nation was the huge amount of gold and other minerals that were discovered there.

The gold rush of the 1850s literally transformed the destiny of Australia and the Aborigines. Prior to the discovery of gold, Europeans could scarcely be talked into settling on the southern continent. Australia was still viewed at that time as an inhospitable land, suitable only for convicts and soldiers. The gold rush, according to historians, marked the end of Australia as a penal colony and its beginning as a nation. The influx of settlers and prospectors that occurred in the last half of the nineteenth century helped seal the fate of the Aborigines.

---

inal reserves were no better than American slums—and often worse.

Many houses were totally unsuited for even substandard living. There was no insulation to keep out the intense heat of the summer or to keep the Aborigines warm in the winter. There was no electricity, no running water, and little effort made toward sanitation. Roofs often leaked, creating a damp, cold, and unhealthy place to live.

Most reserves were terribly overcrowded, making for a quick and easy spread of illness. The clothing that was donated for the Aborigines to wear was totally inadequate. In the late twentieth century, many of these reserves were later ruled "inhumane" and were closed and condemned. The Aborigines who lived there were sent into nearby towns, where living conditions were even worse.

Schooling on the reserves was totally inadequate. The reserve manager's wife, who was not a trained teacher as a rule, usually taught classes. Rather than learning to read and write, the Aborigines were taught instead how to perform manual labor.

Aboriginal Protection Boards

By the year 1900 every state in Australia had passed a protection act that set out rules for how the Aborigines could live. Aboriginal Protection Boards were set up to enforce these rules. Many of them continued to operate until the year 1969. These boards decided where the Aborigines could live, whom they could marry, and how their children were to be raised. The boards also determined what jobs the natives could have and where and when they could travel and whom they could visit. If native workers did not satisfy an employer, the board could also withhold their wages for indefinite periods of time.

In 1965 Queensland passed the Aboriginal and Torres Strait Islander Affairs Act. This act gave the state even more power over the natives. An Aborigine, for instance, could be detained for up to a year "for behaving in an offensive, threatening, insolent, insulting, disorderly, obscene or indecent manner or leaving, escaping, or attempting to leave or escape from the reserve."[71]

Many of the legal restrictions continued as late as 1971. Under the Queensland Aborigine Act, passed in that same year, Aboriginal cultural customs were banned. Censorship of reading matter, mail, and recreation was continued. The government also maintained control of Aboriginal marital and sexual relationships by telling the natives whom they could marry and how many children they could have.

Removal of Aboriginal Children

For Aboriginal historians,

The greatest assault on indigenous cultures and family life was the forced separation or taking away of indigenous children from their families. This occurred in every Australian state from the late 1800's until the practice was officially ended in 1969. During this time, as many as one hundred thousand children were separated from their families.[72]

This policy of removing Aboriginal children from their homes went by many names, as CBS newsman Barry Peterson explains: "assimilation, forced removal, welfare board. . . . Its goal was simple: separate Aborigine children from their families and their heritage, mix them into the Caucasian population, eradicate the Aborigines as a race, [and] create an Australia that was all white."[73]

As the twentieth century opened, the majority of government officials in Australia believed that the full-blooded tribal Aborigines represented a dying race. With Aboriginal numbers dropping rapidly, most experts agreed that within the next twenty years the natives would be extinct. The problem, as the government saw it, was the large number of half-caste children who had a white father and an Aboriginal mother.

At the time these programs were instituted, the ideas of eugenics were very popular across the world. According to writer Robert Manne, "Eugenics taught that one of the responsibilities of the contemporary state was to improve a nation's racial state by breeding programs . . . the breeding out of color."[74] One supporter of this view was anthropologist Herbe Basedow, who wrote: "The Australian Aborigine stands somewhere near the bottom rung of the great evolutionary ladder. . . . A program of controlled breeding out of half-castes . . . [had every prospect] of turning part-Aborigines into whites."[75]

The Stolen Generation

It was the Aboriginal Ordinance Act of 1918 that officially allowed the government to take native children from their families. Taking the children turned out to be an easy task because until the 1960s Aboriginal parents did not even have legal custody of their own children. The children were, instead, considered "wards of the state" and could be taken out of a home at any time, for any reason.

Some of the children were taken at birth, others during their childhood years, and still others while teenagers. Lorraine Mafi-Williams of the Knarkbaul clan was one of the thousands of children taken. Many years later she wrote: "I was twelve years old when we were stolen from our parents. . . . There was no warning. The white welfare officer came in his truck with two white policemen. . . . I was put onto the open-air back of a truck with my brothers and sisters."[76] Aboriginal activist Jack Beetson reported, "It was a green truck that used to come out. It had a big cage in the back of the truck. They'd throw fruit and stuff on the truck. The Aborigine children would jump in. They'd shut the gate and take off."[77]

In Western Australia, James Isdall was one of those responsible for picking up the children. His comments reflect the attitude then prevalent, though not universal, among white Australians. In the mid-twentieth century, he explained: "I would not hesitate for one moment to separate one half-caste from its Aborigine mother, no matter how frantic her momentary grief might be at that time.

An Outcry from White Australians

During the last two hundred years, most white Europeans either supported or ignored the atrocities that were committed against the Aborigines. There was, however, a small group of settlers and citizens who were outraged by what was happening.

All across the continent, sympathetic men and women fought to stop the abusive treatment of the Aborigines. Their voices were few, and those who did speak out often suffered repercussions in the form of violence for their unpopular stands.

Even in the late twentieth century, white Australians who befriended or supported the Aborigines were often the victims of violence. In "A Young Aborigine," which appeared in *Time International* in 1991, Karen Kissane reveals that not all racist activity is against the Aborigines. She quotes Barbara Brady of New South Wales, who had publicly spoken out against the discrimination against the natives. Brady later told a federal commission: "I was the target of obscene phone calls and shotgun blasts over my house."

Schools for the Stolen Generation

Cootamundra Girls' Home was established in 1911. The Aboriginal girls who were taken there were most often trained as domestic servants and sent to work for middle-class white families. According to Aboriginal historians, the girls were instructed "to think white, look white and act white." These girls were taught to fear Aboriginal men and to look down on their own people.

Kinchela, an area of land on the coast of New South Wales, was opened in 1924 as a reserve for young Aborigine boys. Conditions there and at other reserves and orphanages were harsh. Boys typically worked long hours on dairy farms and were often beaten.

Children were taught English and punished for speaking their native tongues. No communication was allowed with their biological families. When the children "graduated," they were sent into towns and small communities, where they were expected to make a living. Most ended up on welfare and many became alcoholics. Not accepted by the white community and not knowing about their Aboriginal roots, many wandered endlessly searching for a sense of belonging.

They soon forget their offspring."[78] Jim Brooks, who has worked with the Aborigine for many years, reports that "[government workers] sincerely believed that indigenous people were somehow immune to normal human emotions."[79] The pain that these removals caused to both parents and children were thus explained as being in the best interest of the children. The real consequences were far different.

Consequences

When the welfare officers came to take three-year-old Archie Roach from his home, they told his mother that they were taking him to a picnic. Instead, he was placed in an institution in Melbourne, where he was later told that his parents had died in a fire. Thousands of Aboriginal children were told similar stories—that their parents were either dead or that their parents didn't want them anymore. The children, with no proof to the contrary, grew up believing these stories. They had no knowledge of their Aboriginal names, culture, or history.

The consequences of forced removal continue to plague the Australian Aborigines even today. Suicide, alcoholism, substance abuse, and shattered families and communities continue to cause problems for the members of this "Stolen Generation" and their families. The story of their abuse, suffering, and lost identity has long been Australia's dirty secret.

Prejudice and the World Wars

Until 1967 the federal government of Australia refused to include the Aborigines as part of their national census. They "did not, in other words," writes Bill Bryson, "count them as people."[80] Aborigines were not considered citizens, could not vote, own property, or hold any kind of government office. They had virtually no control over any aspect of their lives.

Systematic efforts to wipe out their culture have caused widespread destitution and despair among Aborigines.

An example of their near total helplessness was evident in the January 1938 reenactment of the British landing in Sydney. This was part of the celebration held for the 150th anniversary of European settlement. Aboriginal people were trucked into Sydney and actually threatened with starvation if they didn't play their roles in the production.

This prejudice against the Aborigines was also evident during World War I when the hundreds of Aborigines who volunteered for service in the Australian army were turned down. This refusal stemmed from the Australian Defense Act of 1909 that excluded anyone who was "not substantially of European descent." During World War II, the army did accept half-castes into service, but continued to turn down full-blooded Aborigines. The Australian air force, however, did utilize a few Aborigines who went on to play important roles in various reconnaissance units.

Another exception to this policy occurred in northern Australia after the Japanese bombed the town of Darwin in the Northern Territory. This was the first attack on Australian soil by a foreign power and has often been called Australia's Pearl Harbor. As a result of the bombing, a special commando unit made up of Australian soldiers and local Aborigines was formed in 1942. This group used horses and

An Aboriginal elder accompanies the commanding officer of Norforce, one of the Australian army's three regional surveillance units.

canoes along with Aboriginal bush skills to patrol the coastline. Searching for Japanese landings, the commando unit played a key role in the defense of Australia. When the war was over, the regular army members received pensions and medals. The Aborigines received nothing.

Despite their negative experience in the war, Aborigines today continue to cooperate in the defense of their country. An army reserve commando unit, called Norforce, includes volunteer Aborigines from local tribes. The unit guards and patrols Australia's far northern coast, where they practice military techniques while living off the land.

Nuclear Testing

During the 1950s Great Britain conducted a series of atomic bomb testings and explosions on the Maralinga tribe's homeland in South Australia. No one consulted the Maralingas about using this land for the testing. This was considered unnecessary by the government.

The authorities, instead, claimed that prior to the detonations, patrol officers had ensured that there were no Aborigines anywhere near the bombing sites. The British army had also posted "keep out" signs all around the area. Most of the Aborigines, however, could not read English. No one knows for sure how many Aborigines died or suffered ill effects from the testing. "It was all hushed up,"[81] according to author Bruce Chatwin.

An official inquiry into the twelve bombs that fell in the 1950s was finally held in the 1980s. The report stated that, contrary to what was formerly believed, radioactive fallout had landed in areas where the Aborigines lived. The natives fully support this finding. According to Sarina Singh, "Yami Lester is a Yankunytjatjara man who was a child when one of the British nuclear devices was detonated. As a result of radioactive fallout, Yami saw many of his relatives sicken and die; some years later, he [himself] went blind."[82]

Toward the end of the twentieth century, the British government agreed to pay the Aborigines a total of $30 million in damages. This sum, which the Aborigines feel is inadequate compensation for their losses, has yet to be fully paid.

The Policy of Assimilation

The policy of assimilation gained wide support after World War II. According to

The Story of Archie Roach

Archie Roach was one of the Aboriginal children taken from his family and institutionalized in a Melbourne orphanage. Archie's first two foster family experiences failed miserably. The second family abused him so badly that the case ended up in court. The third family, the Cox family of Melbourne, treated Archie fairly, but the boy continued to be miserable. When Roach was fourteen, he received a letter from his up-to-then-unknown sister, telling him of his mother's death. Having been told his parents had died years before, Archie was furious when he realized that he had been lied to for his entire life.

He ran away from the foster home and spent the next twelve years drinking and sleeping in one park after another. Roach finally made an attempt to put his life back together again. He began writing and singing songs. His 1987 hit, "Took the Children Away," is a moving song about his experiences as a child. The song was a nationwide hit and launched Roach on a promising musical career.

Despite his success, Archie Roach is still angry about the past. In 2000 he told *Time* reporter Terry McCarthy: "I still feel the pain, every day. Sometimes it threatens to engulf me. But I'm not going to let it destroy me." The *Time* article entitled "The Stolen Generation" focuses on the former children's plight and their need for an apology from the Australian government—an apology that has yet to happen.

the Koori, a group of Aborigines in New South Wales, "This was defined . . . in practical terms, that during the course of time, it is expected that all persons of Aboriginal blood or mixed blood will live like white Australians do." In 1951 assimilation was adopted as Australia's federal policy. The Koori explain, "To facilitate this process, all Aboriginal people were declared wards, which gave the government legal rights over their movements, employment, residences, wages."[83] In reality, this policy was no different than the earlier protection acts that had controlled the Aborigines' way of life.

By the late 1960s, the government began to question the assimilation process, whose framers had unrealistically assumed that the Aborigines would easily and enthusiastically adopt the "superior" values of the white majority. The legislation had clearly failed to accomplish its purpose. Rather than than changing their ways, most Aborigines had proved to be remarkably steadfast in their refusal to give up their traditional values and practices.

Self-Determination

From a stance calling for assimilation, the federal government of Australia moved somewhat reluctantly to a policy of Aboriginal self-determination. This new policy was defined as "Aboriginal communities deciding the pace and natures of their future development."[84] In 1980, for instance, in much of northern Australia, the federal government purchased many of the Aboriginal reserves and religious missions and turned them over to local natives. This new Aboriginal land was to be administered by land councils controlled by local natives.

Despite this new "ownership" of the land, white interests continued to take precedence. In 1976 the Aboriginal Land Trust Commission bought the Noonkanbah Station for the Yungngora Aborigines. The natives began the work of revitalizing the station under their management.

In 1978 the community learned that an exploration company was planning to drill for oil on areas of the land that was sacred to them. They appealed to the government. After court action, the Western Australian government ruled that the mining could proceed but that the sacred sites were to be protected and avoided by the miners.

The drilling company failed to abide by this ruling. In response, the Yungngora blocked access to the site. In 1980 the drillers were forced to leave, but one year later they returned with full government backing. Police escorts accompanied the workers, and many Aborigines were arrested. The drilling proceeded, although no oil was ever found.

Two Histories in Australia

According to writer Terry McCarthy,

Australia has two separate histories—one white, one black. The former is of a difficult but ultimately successful settlement of a harsh continent, of the exploitation of rich agricultural and mineral resources,

Protests by Aborigine activists have pressured Australia's government to rethink its policies concerning Aboriginal rights.

of the creation of a hardy, no-nonsense social structure. . . . The black version is quite different—one of dispossession of the land after forty thousand years of stewardship, of racial prejudice, victimization . . . and social decay.[85]

Until perhaps the last ten years, most whites in Australia had a blind spot about the real history of their country. As re-

cently as the early 1960s, Queensland schools were using a textbook that "likened Aborigines to feral jungle creatures."[86] Other history books wrote that the Aborigines were cannibals and that women often ate their own babies.

The real story is only now beginning to be told. And only in the last twenty years have some of the abuses of the past been brought to light.

Chapter 6

Aboriginal Life in Modern Australia

Despite many improvements in their standard of living in recent years, it is still a hardship to be an Aborigine in Australia. As the nation begins the twenty-first century, basic needs such as decent health care, education, housing, and employment opportunities are still far from reality for many Aboriginal communities.

Racism

Most, if not all, of the problems facing the Aborigines today are due to the racism and discrimination that exist in modern Australia. Racism is a daily experience for many Aborigines. According to Bill Jonas of the Australian Human Rights and Equal Opportunities Commission, "Racism . . . is an enormous and ongoing problem."[87] Writer Margo Daly agrees with this assessment, saying: "This is a country where racism is ingrained."[88]

A poll taken at the end of the twentieth century showed, despite strong evidence to the contrary, that over half of the Australian population believed that the Abo-

rigines were being treated too generously. The natives today still arouse pity and disgust among many white Australians. As an Australian told travel writer Paul Theroux, "I'm not a racist. I just hate Aborigines."[89] Aborigines throughout the country are still referred to by offensive nicknames—"coons," "boongs," "bings," and "murkys." These names are all racial slurs and continue to be used by large numbers of Australians.

According to Dr. Rosemary van den Berg:

There are still people . . . in Australia who refuse to acknowledge Aboriginal existence. . . . I am an Elder of the *Nyoongar* people . . . and I . . . have found that there are white . . . Australians who will not talk to an Aboriginal person unless it is absolutely necessary. . . . I have found that only the most daring will sit next to an Aboriginal person on public transport. Shopkeepers . . . usually ignore an Aboriginal person waiting to be served. Public hospitals . . . make Aboriginal people wait longer than others to see the doctor.[90]

When writer Marlo Morgan visited Australia in the 1980s, she was shocked to find how widespread the racism actually was. She asked a new Australian acquaintance, an educated man, about the situation. His response amazed and appalled her:

Yes, it's sad. But nothing can be done. You don't understand the abos . . . they are primitive, wild, bush people. We have offered to educate them. . . . In the past they were cannibals. Now they still do not want to turn loose of their customs and old beliefs. . . . They are hopelessly illiterate people with no ambition. . . . After two hundred years, they still don't fit in. What's more, they don't

Online in the Outback

Communications between isolated Aboriginal communities have always been difficult. For a number of these remote settlements, video conferencing has become the main method used for personal, business, and government communication.

The Tanami Network in Australia's Northern Territory came into existence in 1993 and is owned and operated exclusively by the Warlpiri Aborigines. A computer-video system connects four different Warlpiri communities with the cities of Alice Springs, Sydney, and Darwin. The network is widely used to provide access to government service groups and business contacts for Warlpiri businesses. It also enables the Aborigines to obtain adult education, teacher training, remote health care, and legal assistance.

In addition to providing these services, the Tanami Network allows the Warlpiri to communicate with their extended family and friends. This kind of communication has helped to overcome the isolation found in small rural communities. Families from different communities, for example, conduct regular reunions by simply gathering in front of a television monitor.

Perhaps the most exciting use of the system is the conferences that are being held between the Warlpiri and indigenous groups on other continents. These video conferences have so far focused primarily on land rights and language preservation. But one session in the late twentieth century allowed an exchange of native dances with members of the Little Red Cree Indian Nation of Canada.

try. . . . Believe me, there is nothing you can do to inspire them.[91]

As she traveled throughout Australia, Morgan found these characterizations to be totally false.

Violations of Human Rights

In 1988 a report from the United Nations warned that Australia's treatment of the Aborigines violated the natives' basic human rights. Says a Yorta Yorta woman, Karen Milward: "Aboriginal people have to deal with racist attitudes at many levels. I have encountered racism from a former boss who told me that I was 'not bad looking for a boong.' . . . Later he sarcastically said, 'Nice scarf you're wearing, did you steal it?'"[92]

The Australian media do little to offset the negative viewpoint that white Australians have of Aborigines. In 1990 the National Inquiry into Racist Violence found that the Aborigines, themselves, believed that television and newspapers played a major role in the ongoing racism. The inquiry supported this belief and concluded that the media displayed Aboriginal people in a predominantly negative way. Aboriginal-based media organizations are now working to change this representation.

This woman makes a home of an abandoned prison. Overcrowding, unemployment, and discrimination have made her predicament common among Australia's Aboriginal population.

Redfern

In the middle of the city of Sydney, a group of Aborigines took over the slums and turned them into the native community of Redfern. This unique community began in the 1930s during the Great Depression, when Aboriginal workers and their families moved to the city in search of jobs. At that time Redfern was the cheapest, dirtiest, and most run-down section of Sydney. It was also the only place in the city where the Aborigines were allowed to live.

By the late 1960s, Redfern began to attract middle-class and intellectual Aborigines. Among those who came were writers, poets, artists, and politicians. It wasn't long before the slums of Redfern became the center of Aboriginal cultural life in Sydney.

During the last thirty years, Redfern has improved in many ways. The area had for years been characterized by row after row of falling-down houses. In recent years the Aborigines have adapted and remodeled their homes. Whole interiors were rebuilt to suit the needs of large extended families. Terraces and porches were built and then painted in the red and white ocher colors of the desert. Brightly painted murals replaced the grimy dark bricks of the once-nasty slum. Large community areas were added along with outdoor parks and playgrounds.

In Redfern today the Aborigines have pride in what they've created. Here the natives run their own schools, radio stations, theater groups, housing authority, and legal services. Children are taught their own language and culture by Aboriginal teachers.

Incarceration

Nowhere is the discrimination against Aborigines more apparent than in the number of natives put in jail. Very few Aborigines live their entire lives without coming into direct contact with the police or the courts of Australia. The statistics are alarming. In the Northern Territory, for example, 70 percent of all prisoners are Aborigines. In the nation as a whole, the natives are sixteen times more likely to be in prison and sixty times more likely to be arrested than the rest of the population.

One reason for this high rate of imprisonment has been the racial attitudes that exist among police forces all over the continent. Even when independent witnesses testify about police brutality or improper arrests, most courts and juries rule against the Aborigines. To make matters worse, in the past the natives have generally had inadequate or no legal representation.

Many Aborigines are arrested for offenses like causing a public disturbance or drunkenness. According to a report from the Royal Commission in 1990 that looked into Aboriginal arrests, white Australians were far less likely to be imprisoned for the same offenses: "[The Aborigines'] imprisonment rate is directly related to their [being black]."[93] This report also offered testimony given by many Aboriginal inmates. Many of them reported unjustified strip searches. Others spoke of being thrown naked into punishment cells with concrete floors and no blankets.

Since the formation of the Aboriginal Legal Service in the late twentieth century, some Aborigines are faring a little better in court. Aboriginal and non-Aboriginal lawyers are now working together to help make sure that the natives who are charged with crimes at least have adequate legal representation.

Prison Deaths

If the number of arrests of Aborigines is disproportionately high, the number of deaths among Aboriginal prisoners is alarming. During the late 1980s and early 1990s, Aborigines died in prison at the rate of one every two weeks. The Royal Commission again pointed to racism as the most significant contributing factor for native deaths while in custody. According to writer Ken Edwards, "While the police had not murdered the Aborigines in their custody, the commission found that often callous neglect by the officers had led to many of the deaths."[94]

Until the nineteenth century, the Aborigines had no concept of imprisonment. Prison has been so alien to the natives that they simply don't know how to handle it.

Theroux states: "A jail cell is an Aborigine's idea of hell on earth."[95] Young Aborigines are simply terrified when imprisoned in isolated and confined areas. Many are so afraid that death is seen as the only way out.

Health Problems

Life expectancy among the Aborigines is fifteen years shorter than that of the average white Australian. Aborigines also suffer in alarming numbers from heart disease, tuberculosis, hepatitis, and diabetes. The rates for these diseases and others among the native population far exceed the national average. Infant mortality, for instance, is nineteen deaths among every one thousand Aboriginal births. This compares very unfavorably with the white rate of five infant deaths per one thousand births.

Many of the health problems that affect the Aborigines today can be traced to inadequate housing, poor water quality, and deplorable sanitation. These factors all seriously impact the health of the natives, particularly their children. In addition, many Aborigines live in isolated communities where regular medical service is not available. In these areas the natives must be prepared to treat many common illnesses, snakebites, and broken bones themselves. In the past, native doctors were well equipped to deal with these problems in a natural way. Unfortunately, much of this ancient knowledge has been lost. Efforts are now being made to record and publish the Aborigines' remaining knowledge of traditional medicine.

Another factor contributing to the health problems among the Aborigines

An Aborigine woman and child stand outside a health clinic. In recent years Australia's government has begun to address the alarming health problems among Aborigines.

health services for the Aborigines had been totally provided and administered by white medical professionals who often could not understand their patients or their peculiar problems. As Australia begins the twenty-first century, according to writer Robyn Davidson, "the more enlightened [white] health workers are now working hand in hand with native doctors and midwives in trying to cope with various diseases and ailments that affect Aborigines."[96]

Despite recent advances in health care for the Aborigines, the situation remains critical. Activist Jack Beetson, who is the executive director of Tranby Aboriginal College, writes: "If the health of all Australia was the same [as the Aborigines] we would be declared a national disaster."[97]

has been the drastic change in diet that has occurred over the past two hundred years. In these contemporary times, Aborigines eat a wide range of junk food that contains large amounts of sugar and fat. Obesity, diabetes, and heart problems, in particular, can be traced to this change in diet.

In 1989 the first comprehensive National Aboriginal Health Strategy was put in place by the Australian government. Up until the late twentieth century,

Alcoholism

Alcoholism has become a significant problem for the Aborigines. According to writer Linda Christmas, "They drink to forget the loss of their traditional ways and the irreparable damage done to their culture . . . ; they drink because they are a conquered people . . . ; everything they cherish has been taken from them."[98] Writer James Cowan agrees with this assessment and adds: "Sadly, for many Aborigines, the Dream Journey as a ritual act has instead found its substitute in alcohol."[99]

Alice Springs has often been referred to as the alcoholic capital of Australia. Its citizens (black and white) consume two and a half times as much alcohol as the national average. While many whites drink excessively, the problem among the Aborigines is particularly alarming. According to reporters who have visited the area, many of the natives lie in an alcoholic stupor during most of the day.

The problem is worsened by the fact that the long-term effects of alcohol abuse seem to be far worse for the Aborigines than for all but a handful of white Australians. Sci-entists now believe that these devastating effects are caused by a lack of zinc in the natives' livers. Christmas says simply, "The white man has had generations to lick his liver into shape and build up resistance [to alcohol]; the Aborigine has not."[100]

Many Aboriginal leaders are well aware of the dangers and damage the natives are doing to themselves. They have begun to ban alcohol at the outstations and settlements where they live. Tribal leaders are beginning to impose heavy fines on those who are found drinking or bringing liquor into the communities.

The Outstation Movement

Since the early 1970s, small groups of Aboriginal people have been moving away from the cities, towns, and large settlements to establish "outstation" communities in the Outback. This movement reflects a desire by the natives to reaffirm their links with the land and their traditional culture.

Mark Moora has led a group of his people away from the Aboriginal community of Balgo in the Kimberley area of Australia. Quoted from Harvey Arden's *National Geographic* article, "Journey Into Dreamtime," Moora says: "Had to get away from Balgo. Too many people there. Too noisy. So about thirty of us came here. We call it *Yagga Yagga*. . . . It means 'quiet, quiet.'"

The Aborigines who live on the Daly River Reserve in the Northern Territory also still follow their ancient customs. Every year during the rainy season, the natives disappear into the Outback on an annual walkabout. They may be gone as long as three months, during which time the Aborigines shed their clothing and live as their ancestors did hundreds of years ago.

Many of the strongest and most successful Aboriginal communities, in fact, are to be found in remote places out of sight of modern society. In these areas elders maintain strict discipline among the clans and follow many of the old traditional ways.

Lack of Education

Many white teachers still label Aboriginal children as backward because the young people find it difficult to understand, much less speak, read, or write English. Most native children are placed at the bottom of the class even before the first tests are taken.

Unfortunately, white schools are the only schools available for many Aboriginal children. Their home life creates additional problems. "Many of these children are bawled out for not doing homework," writes Davidson, who visited a school and community in the Outback. "Yet is it possible to do homework when home [for these children] is a rusted-out car body?"[101]

Another problem for the Aborigines is the high percentage of students who drop out of school at an early age. School, these students discover, offers them little they need to know, especially since the only jobs many of them are likely to get is as low-paid workers on the sheep and cattle stations. This kind of work, they realize, does not require the ability to read and write. During the 1980s over two-thirds of all Aboriginal students left school before the age of sixteen.

There are many special programs now available for Aboriginal children in modern Australia. Many schools have hired a special native teacher's aide who speaks the local native dialects. The aide's job is to help the children in the classroom as they begin to learn English.

In Western Australia an Aboriginal elder named Ken Colbung started an all-native school called Ngangara. At this school Aboriginal students first learn about their own culture and history before they even attempt to learn English and other subjects. Colbung's school has proven a great success, and many of his students have gone on to graduate from the public school system.

The Australian government is also responding to the high dropout rate among native children. Many Aboriginal families are now receiving a special monetary allowance to help buy school clothes and other necessities.

Employment Opportunities

It was not until the 1940s that the Aborigines began to receive any monetary pay for their work efforts on the great sheep and cattle stations in the Outback. Those Aborigines who had moved to towns and cities during the Great Depression fared little better. Most found themselves stuck in one or another poorly paid job. Many natives became dependent on welfare programs offered by charity organizations and the federal government, and, indeed, welfare still forms the main income for many Aborigines living in remote and rural communities. As the twenty-first century opened, the unemployment rate for Aborigines was an alarming 26 percent as compared with 8 percent for the general community.

In the last twenty years in Australia, the job situation has improved somewhat for the Aborigines. Many natives continue to find employment at the numerous sheep and cattle stations that fill the interior of Australia. These Aborigines often play an important role at the ranches due to their uncanny ability to find water and to stop stampedes by "singing" to the cattle.

The introduction of Aboriginal positions within many governmental departments and organizations has also recently resulted in an increase in the employment of native people. In addition, Aborigines are now beginning to play an active role in environmental and conservation programs. According to Tjapuka Aborigine Barry Hunter, "Although much of the special knowledge of the environment has been lost . . . a great deal still exists. . . . Many Aborigines . . . want to play a role in managing their country. . . . Australia . . . needs Aboriginal people and their knowledge to play a role in environmental management."[102]

Business Ownership

The Aborigines, with few exceptions, have had little success in owning and running their own small businesses. Raising money is a very difficult proposition for the natives. Australian banks have been historically reluctant to loan money to those Aboriginal people interested in opening businesses. As a result, most of the loans must be obtained from government service agencies or Aboriginal community organi-

A rancher herds cattle in Australia's interior. Some ranches benefit from the Aborigines' unique knowledge of land and animals.

Tent Embassy

The Aboriginal "Tent Embassy" was established on the lawns of the Old Parliament House in Canberra on January 26, 1972. The Aborigines purposefully called this gathering an "embassy" because they wanted to symbolize the fact that most of the indigenous people feel that they are treated as foreigners in their own country. The Tent Embassy provided a focus for the Aborigines' campaign for land rights and social justice. It also served as a meeting place for all people interested in native issues.

On a number of occasions, Canberra police forcibly evicted the Aborigines from this site, but each time the embassy was rebuilt. It remained in place until 1975, when the Aborigines temporarily removed it. In 1992, when the land rights issue once again made headlines, the Tent Embassy was reestablished in the same place. It is still there today.

zations. Even these are often hesitant to help fund native business ventures.

Low levels of formal education also work against Aboriginal ownership of small businesses. Despite recent advances in the availability of educational opportunities, there are still very limited numbers of Aboriginal lawyers, accountants, and professional business advisers in Australia.

Moreover, goals other than making money are considered more important among many native societies. For the Aborigines, family relationships, social obligations, and the preservation of the tribe's cultural identity take precedence over commercial success.

Finally, according to journalist Michael Schaper, "The remote locations of many Aboriginal communities also mitigate against business creation. Many Aborig-

ines live in relatively small and isolated localities in the Outback. Transport costs are high, communication is sometimes difficult and the pool of both consumers and skilled labor is small."[103]

All of these factors make it difficult for the Aborigines to invest in and prosper in the business world. The one area where the natives do appear to be making an impact is the tourist trade. Aboriginal-run tour groups are beginning to take some real steps forward in bringing profits to their communities. There are also expanding opportunities for native artists and craftsmen.

An example of a well-run and profitable business is the large community cattle and sheep reserve of Utopia. As Davidson writes: "I spent several weeks at Utopia, a beautiful rich 170-square-mile

Like nearly 40 percent of his fellow Aborigines, this man lives in poverty.

cattle property which has been given over to the Aboriginal people. . . . Contrary to negative press reports, they are managing the property very well."[104]

Another example of native success is the Bima Wear textile factory run by the Tiwi natives of Melville Island. Today the factory produces curtains, towels, and other fabrics in distinctive native designs.

Poverty

Despite advances, many Aborigines still live in dire poverty. Recent statistics, for example, indicate that nearly 40 percent of all Aborigines live in poverty, as compared with 2 percent for white Australians. Even among those natives who work, their weekly income is over a hundred dollars less a week than the average white Australian's.

In Alice Springs many of the Aborigines are so poor that they eat from garbage cans or discarded food they find at trash dumps. In March 1988 a report by Britain's Anti-Slavery Society stated: "Australia's Aborigines live in conditions comparable to the worst third world slum."[105]

Australia has one of the highest standards of living in the world, but Aborigines in the twenty-first century still occupy the lowest position in just about every aspect of society.

Chapter 7

Hope for the Future

The 1960s were a time of radical change all over the world. The civil rights movement in the United States made international headlines, and the fight against discrimination affected indigenous cultures around the world. In Australia there were sit-ins, strikes, and other impressive demonstrations. All of these protests were intended to bring the racist policies against the Aborigines to the awareness of the entire country. These initial actions were also aimed at regaining title to native lands lost when the Europeans landed in 1788.

In 1965 Dr. Kumantjayi Perkins brought together a busload of university students and traveled throughout New South Wales. The Aboriginal group's political trip came to be known as the Australian Freedom Ride. And in 1966 over two hundred stockmen, domestic workers, and their families walked off the Wave Hill Cattle Station in the Northern Territory. The natives were demanding better wages and working conditions. It would be nearly twenty years later before some of the Wave Hill work-

ers' requests for fair wages were met. But the stage had been set for even more noteworthy events.

Land Rights

The Aboriginal struggle for reclaiming their land goes back to the earliest days of the European occupation of Australia. From the time the first Aborigines were pushed off their land, the natives have protested in one way or another. The land—the core of Aboriginal life and spirituality—is central to nearly every issue that is important to the natives today. As the Aborigines enter the twenty-first century, they continue to not only fight for their land but also for recognition of their way of life.

According to author John Pilger:

From time to time, Australian politicians rediscover the indigenous population and announce solutions to the "problem." In the 1980's, Bob Hawke [prime minister of Australia], the tears welling in his eyes,

In the 1980s, Australian prime minister Bob Hawke pledged to return land taken from Aborigines, but failed to follow through on his promise.

promised repeatedly to right the historic wrongs . . . then abandoned all pretense of a land rights' policy in the face of a campaign by the mining companies.[106]

Other politicians have also promised action but have failed to follow through. The pressure from mining companies and cattle and sheep owners has been enough to sway political votes. Australia's economy depends on the export of beef and lamb and also on the immense riches from diamond and other mining ventures. Thus, many

white Australians, legislators and voters alike, fear that if the Aborigines regain large portions of land, there will be economic devastation, at least in the short term.

The Mabo Ruling

In 1992 the High Court of Australia issued a landmark ruling that, for the first time in that country's history, supported the Aborigines' claim that "we were here first." This ruling stated that the continent of Australia had not, in fact, been *terra nullius,* or "land belonging to no one," when Captain James Cook sailed into Sydney Harbor. The ruling went on to state that the Aborigines had been wrongly displaced from their land and that, as a result, the natives were entitled to file suit to reclaim that land.

This momentous ruling had come about because of a lawsuit brought by Eddie Mabo, a community leader and human rights activist, and four other Torres Strait Islander natives in 1982. Mabo and the others claimed that their home island of Met (Murray Island) had been continuously inhabited and possessed by their ancestors. Therefore, they proclaimed, the Islanders were the true owners of the island.

After considering the evidence, the High Court finally ruled on the case ten years later. On June 3, 1992, the court handed down its decision in *Mabo v. the State of Queensland.* To the dismay and shock of the government, the court ruled that the denial of native property rights based on the principles of *terra nullius* was not only wrong, but racist.

This ruling opened the door for Aborigines all over Australia to file lawsuits proclaiming their own rights to land. The indigenous people of the Northern Territory have had the most success in regaining title to their homeland. As of the late 1990s, more than 25 percent of the Territory's land had been returned to Aboriginal families and tribes. An additional 25 percent has been claimed, but these cases are still pending.

Largely because of this significant court decision, in 1993 the Australian Parliament passed the Native Title Act. This act gives compensation to those Aborigines who have been driven from their homelands. It also attempts to listen to the claims of miners and farmers who currently live on Aboriginal land.

The "Bringing Them Home Report"

Pressure from Aboriginal organizations finally forced the Australian government to investigate the old policy of removing native children from their homes. In 1997 an official inquiry by the Human Rights and Equal Opportunities Commission produced a document called the "Bringing Them Home

The Wik Decision

In 1996 the High Court of Australia made an important ruling that has come to be known as the Wik decision. In this case the court ruled that Aboriginal title to the land could coexist with mining and farming leases. This meant that Aborigines could enter certain areas to hold ceremonies or gather bush foods as long as they did nothing to disturb the farming or mining land.

This ruling created an uproar among many white communities. The governments of many Australian states see the Wik decision as a big threat to their economic interests. Already mining companies have expressed their reluctance to invest in land that might be affected by the court's ruling. The governments of the Northern Territory, Queensland, and Western Australia have mounted a vocal and costly campaign against the Aborigines.

The struggle for land rights continues as the Aborigines and Australia begin the twenty-first century. When John Howard was elected prime minister of Australia in 1996, one of his first actions was to slash the Aboriginal budget by almost one-half. Aboriginal groups have found themselves increasingly under attack from Howard's government and other high-profile groups.

Report." The findings of the commission shocked not only the people of Australia but concerned citizens all around the world.

For the first time, the world became aware of some of the abuses and injustices that had been heaped upon the Aborigines. One in three children, the board reported, had been part of the "Stolen Generation." In addition, according to *Time* reporter Terry McCarthy, "[the] official inquiry found consistent patterns of physical and sexual abuse of the stolen children, of exploitation in the labor market and of social dislocation that led many into alcohol, violence and early death."[107]

An organization called Link-Up was formed to work with Aboriginal adults who had been separated from their families years earlier. This organization continues to provide support and counseling to families who are, for the first time in decades, reuniting. Since its beginnings, Link-Up has worked with thousands of Aborigines.

Australia Day

January 26, 1988, was celebrated throughout the nation as Australia Day. This day marked the two-hundredth anniversary of the first British settlement of the continent. On the very same day, some 200,000 people—black and white—marched across Sydney Harbor Bridge calling for a nationwide reconciliation with the Aborigines. Theirs was not a celebration but rather a display of mourning and remembrance for the losses experienced by the

Aborigines in ceremonial paint turn out in protest of Australia's bicentennial celebration, which commemorated the two-hundredth anniversary of British settlement of the continent.

natives. This was the largest political demonstration in the country's history.

Aborigines from all over Australia commemorated their ancestors as they reminded the nation that the Europeans' achievements had, in fact, caused great suffering among the native peoples. Thousands of miles away on the coast of Dover, England, an Aboriginal elder named Burnam Burnam planted the Aboriginal flag on behalf of his people. In this symbolic action, he announced that he was claiming the entire United Kingdom on behalf of the Aborigines. His statement, while not meant to be taken literally, served to show how ridiculous it had been for the British to arrive in Australia and claim that land as their own.

Keeping Aboriginal Culture Alive

Few white Australians, or whites elsewhere for that matter, took any real interest in the Aborigines until the 1960s. Since that time "Aboriginality" has become a thriving industry, first among archaeologists and anthropologists, and then among the general public.

Ceremonies and art forms that had been forgotten are now being revived through research, while languages that had fallen into disuse are being relearned. Many Aboriginal tour companies are introducing visitors for the first time to ancient lands. These natives are explaining Aboriginal cultural beliefs and sharing the real story of their history. Aboriginal dance theaters are staging new and fascinating produc-

tions and are performing ancient dances for modern audiences.

Today the Aborigines are keeping their culture alive by passing on their knowledge to future generations. They are working tirelessly to protect their sacred and significant sites. These words from Lorraine Mafi-Williams reflect the roles that are being played today by Aboriginal elders: "An Aboriginal elder is a caretaker and keeper of sacred and ancient knowledge that has been passed down many, many generations. . . . Today, a big part of my role as an Elder is to raise awareness about indigenous Australia and to break the old 'noble savage' stereotype that still exists."[108]

Preserving the Languages

In modern Australia only about one-fifth of all Aborigines can speak their native dialect. Many native languages have been lost forever, including the original languages of Tasmania and most of those spoken in New South Wales. An exception to this overall pattern can be found in the Northern Territory, where there are still over forty different indigenous languages spoken. Many Aboriginal cultural groups are now working with older natives who may be the only surviving speakers of a particular dialect. After collecting information about each language, these groups are then teaching others to speak it.

A growing number of indigenous people in Australia dislike the word "Aborigine" because the word carries such negative connotations. Many groups have looked for alternative words to describe themselves. The word "Koori," for example, is used by the majority of Aboriginal tribes in the states of Victoria and New South Wales. The word "Yolngu" is used in the Northern Territory's Arnhem Land, while "Murri" is preferred in much of Queensland. These are but a few examples of the words that have been chosen all over the continent.

Aboriginal Art

Since the 1980s Aboriginal art has enjoyed a real boom and increase in popularity in Australia and around the world. Perhaps the most famous Aboriginal painter was Albert Namatjira (1902–1959). A member of the Aranda tribe, he grew up on a mission near Alice Springs. He used watercolors to portray the scenic beauty of his

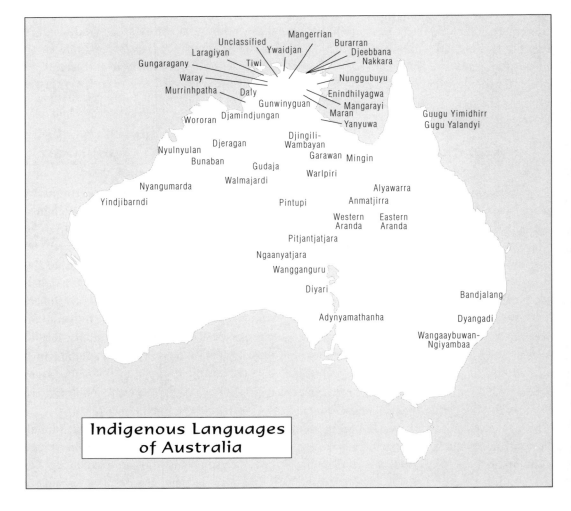

Indigenous Languages of Australia

Australia's Other Indigenous People

The Torres Strait Islanders are Australia's other indigenous people. Arriving on a group of islands between Australia and New Guinea about four thousand years ago, the Islanders are culturally distinct from the Aborigines. The people are Melanesians and are racially related to the indigenous people of New Guinea and a number of other islands in the southern Pacific Ocean.

While different from the Aborigines who live on the mainland, the Torres Strait Islanders, nonetheless, adopted many aspects of Aboriginal culture. They also retained many of their own traditional ways of life. For instance, the Islanders, unlike their mainland neighbors, based their way of life on the sea and stars. They are very much a seafaring people, rather than a people who live off the land. They are connected spiritually with the stars, not the land.

Today the Torres Strait Islands are part of Queensland, which annexed the islands in 1879. The specific needs and identity of the natives there have long been ignored by the Australian government. In 1994, however, a Torres Strait Regional Authority was finally established to deal with native land claims and equality issues.

homeland. His paintings sold quite well throughout the 1940s and 1950s. All of the money that he made went toward helping to improve his tribe's way of life.

Despite Namatjira's fame, he was still subject to the controls of the Aboriginal Protection Boards. In 1951 he was denied permission to build a house for himself. And despite being granted an honorary Australian citizenship in 1957, Namatjira was arrested for sharing alcohol with a family member who was not a citizen. He was subsequently forced to spend two months under arrest on the Papunya Reserve. He died of a heart attack three months later. According to Sarina Singh, "Although Namatjira died of a broken spirit [because] of his ill treatment by white society, his art did much to change white Australia's rather negative view of the Aborigines."[109]

In the 1970s the Aboriginal people living in Papunya in the western desert developed their own school of art. Painting in traditional styles, they sold paintings to art galleries all over Australia. According to writer Carl Robinson, "[Their] paintings . . . which use modern acrylics on canvas to portray ancient legends are [still] in high demand around the world."[110]

Located in Arnhem Land is the Injalak Arts and Crafts Center, a gathering place for Aborigines who live in the area. According to resident artist Leslie Nawirridj,

"In the late 1980's Aborigine artists from this area got together and said they wanted their own place to paint, show and sell their own art. Without Injalak a lot of us would be unemployed."[111] Their artwork has been shown in galleries all over the world.

Aboriginal Dance, Theater, and Film

For the Aborigines, dance and music are centuries-old rituals. One of the best known places where traditional song and dances are performed is the Aboriginal Islander Dance Theatre. Musicians beat out rhythms with ancient instruments, while singers chant special sacred songs, some of which have hundreds of verses.

David Gulpilil is one of Australia's best known actors. A member of the Mandalpingu tribe of Arnhem Land, Gulpilil grew up in a traditional Aboriginal home. Today he is the holder of many of his tribe's secrets, having been initiated as a young man into their ancient rituals and beliefs. In addition to his acting, Gulpilil also teaches the young men of his tribe to hunt and fish in the ancient way. One of his most important contributions to his people is the passing on of songs, ceremonies, and the history of his homeland.

At the Tjapukai Aboriginal Cultural Park in Queensland, the Djabugay Aborigines show a beautiful documentary film. This movie describes the history of the tribe in the native tongue, while being simultaneously translated into seven other languages, including English. In this way, the Aborig-ines of this tribe hope to pass on their cultural history and traditional way of life.

Aboriginal Literature

Today there are a number of newspapers and magazines produced by Aboriginal organizations. One of the most popular is *Deadly Vibes,* based in Sydney. This monthly magazine focuses on indigenous sports, health, and lifestyles.

The first major Aborigine author who wrote in English was Oodgeroo Noonuccal, also known as Kath Walker. Her first volume of poetry, *We are Going,* was published in 1964. Her poems express her concern about the loss of Aboriginal culture and the ensuing struggles that have resulted from the Aborigines being driven off their land. In other published works, Noonuccal voiced her feelings as she pleaded for justice for the natives of Australia. She died in 1992.

Another prominent Aboriginal writer is Ruby Langford. Her book *Don't Take Your Love to Town* deals with the struggle of an Aboriginal woman as she tries to raise a large family by herself. Sally Morgan's *My Place,* according to Singh,

is one of the most popular books ever written by an Aborigine. It's been translated into numerous languages [and is] the story of Morgan's mother and grandmother who try to pass Sally . . . off as something other than an Aborigine in an attempt to evade the government's policy of removing children [from their homes.][112]

Yothu Yindi

The rock group Yothu Yindi, which means "Child and Mother," is an immensely popular group of Aboriginal musicians. Using a blend of ancient rhythms and instruments, along with modern sounds and electric guitars, the band has done much to popularize Aboriginal land rights. Their hit song "Treaty" addresses the broken promises made to the natives and was voted the most popular song in Australia in 1991. The band has appeared throughout Australia and has even performed concerts at Kennedy Center in Washington, D.C.

Mandawuy Yunupingu is the lead singer of this popular group. He was the first Arnhem Land Aborigine to graduate from college, and for many years he worked as a school principal. In 1998 he was awarded an honorary degree from Queensland University in recognition of his contributions to the education of Aboriginal children. The diploma also recognized his songs for the greater understanding they have created between Aborigines and non-Aborigines.

Religion Today

While many indigenous peoples come to share the religious beliefs and values imposed upon them by outsiders, the Aborigines, for the most part, have never truly adopted Christianity. Their beliefs continue to be based on their sense of belonging to the land, to other people, and to their culture. Says Wadjularbinna Doomadgee, who is the leader of the Gungalidda tribe, "Our people [are] very spiritual people. They [are] connected to the land and creation through the great spirit."[113]

The Torres Strait Islanders—who are considered to be Aboriginal people but differ in certain aspects from the mainland Aborigines—did adopt Christianity. The islanders saw the religion as a liberating force and not all that different from many of their traditional beliefs. Most Aboriginal tribes, however, still perform the traditional rituals and religious ceremonies as their ancestors have for hundreds of years.

Hope for the Future

With the recent resurgence in Aboriginal arts, the efforts being made to preserve native cultures, languages, and ways of life, and the advances made in regaining much of their land, the Aborigines look to the future with hope. There is one area, however, where the people feel no progress has been made. They have yet to hear an apology from the Australian government for the abuses of the past. Nor have they ever signed a treaty with the "white men." According to Aboriginal historians, "The Aboriginal people of Australia fought the colonial invasion with honor and they have never surrendered. There is no treaty signifying the cessation of hostilities. From an indigenous viewpoint, the current government of Australia can be seen as the director of an occupational force."[114]

The Barunga Statement of 1988 now hangs in the Parliament building in Canberra. In this document the Aborigines call on Parliament "to negotiate with us a treaty or compact recognizing our prior ownership, continued occupation and sovereignty and affirming our human rights and freedom."[115]

Reconciliation

Reconciliation between the Aborigines and the non-Aboriginal people in Australia is one of the most important issues facing

An Aborigine man and white child stand in front of the "Sea of Hands," a monument symbolizing reconciliation between white and Aboriginal Australians.

Cathy Freeman

Cathy Freeman became a national symbol for all of Australia as she completed the journey of the Olympic Torch in the year 2000. Carrying the flame proudly, she lit the huge Olympic cauldron and stood silently as the ring of fire encircled her. For any Australian, to light the torch would have been a special moment, but Cathy Freeman is an Aborigine. Many observers felt that her selection as flame bearer gave hope to all Aborigines and other Australians that the two racial groups could achieve a peaceful reconciliation.

Cathy's grandmother had been one of the children of the "Stolen Generation." At the age of ten, Cathy, herself, experienced racism. She won five school races, yet received no trophy, while the white runners-up proudly displayed theirs.

Cathy was the first Aborigine to compete in the Olympics and the first to wave her people's flag at a sporting event. During the 1994 Commonwealth Games in Canada, she hoisted the red, black, and yellow banner for her victory lap. The Aborigines had adopted this flag in 1972. In the center is a golden disk that represents the sun, the giver of all life. The top half of the flag is black and stands for the dark-skinned natives. The red bottom represents the earth.

Ten nights after lighting the Olympic Torch in 2000, Cathy Freeman took her place on the starting line for the 400-meter race. When she crossed the finish line forty-nine seconds later, she had won the gold medal for Australia. Many extremists in the country grumbled, but most Australians cheered "Our Cath!" and proudly claimed her as an Australian. Cathy Freeman had become a symbol of hope.

Cathy Freeman, the first Australian Aborigine to compete in the Olympics, carries the Olympic torch in the opening ceremony of the 2000 Summer Olympic Games in Sydney.

the country in the twenty-first century. The goal of reconciliation is to have a united Australia with all of its citizens respecting the land and living in equality with justice for all. Reconciliation would also mean that non-Aborigines value the Aboriginal heritage as well as their own.

By the year 2000, over 250,000 Australians—black and white—had signed thousands of plastic hands, called the Sea of Hands. The hands are planted in the ground on wire stems and have been displayed in every major city on the continent. The group responsible for this idea is Australians for Native Title and Reconciliation. The Sea of Hands is a very graphic way to represent reconciliation between the two races.

In 1992 Prime Minister Paul Keating voiced his own support of reconciliation at the beginning of Australia's celebration of the International Year of the World's Indigenous People, stating:

It might help if we non-Aboriginal Australians imagined ourselves dispossessed of the land we lived on for fifty thousand years, and then imagined ourselves being told it had never been ours. Imagine if ours was the oldest culture in the world and we were told that it was worthless. Imagine if we had resisted this settlement, suffered and died in the defense of our land, and then were told in history books that we had given up without a fight. . . . Imagine if our spiritual life was denied and ridiculed. Imagine if we had suffered injustice and then were blamed for it.[116]

These words reflect the beliefs of the Aborigines and a growing number of supporters. As the new century opened, however, the main obstacle to reconciliation was the reluctance shown by the federal government to push forward with native land rights and the failure of authorities to offer an apology for the past.

The Aborigines, however, remain hopeful that their voices will continue to be heard and that the twenty-first century will bring peace and reconciliation for all the people of Australia.

Notes

Introduction: Who Are the Indigenous People of Australia?

1. Dreaming Online, "Indigenous Australia," www.dreamtime.net.au/indigenous/timeline3.cfm.

Chapter 1: The Land and Its Resources

2. Bill Bryson, *In a Sunburned Country.* New York: Broadway Books, 2000, p. 187.
3. James Cowan, *Mysteries of the Dreamtime: The Spiritual Life of Australian Aborigines.* New South Wales: Unity Press, 1989, pp. 91, 94.
4. Sarina Singh et al., *Aboriginal Australia and the Torres Strait Islanders.* Melbourne: Lonely Planet Publications, 2001, p. 93.
5. Ron Cherry, "Australian Aborigines," June 1993. www.bugbios.com/ced1/aust_abor.html.
6. John H. Chambers, *A Traveler's History of Australia.* New York: Interlink Books, 1999, p. 17.
7. Dreaming Online, "Indigenous Australia."
8. Quoted in Scott Forbes, *Australian Outback.* Singapore: Discovery Communications, 2000, p. 101.
9. Bryson, *In a Sunburned Country,* p. 173.

Chapter 2: The Dreamtime

10. Marlo Morgan, *Mutant Message Down Under.* New York: Harper Perennial, 1991, p. 51.
11. Bruce Chatwin, *The Songlines.* New York: Penguin Books, 1987, p. 11.
12. Robyn Davidson, *Tracks.* New York: Vintage Books, 1980, p. 172.
13. Quoted in Singh, *Aboriginal Australia,* p. 107.
14. Johanna Lambert, *Wise Women of the Dreamtime.* Rochester, VT: Inner Traditions International, 1993, p. 5.
15. National Geographic editors, *Enduring Treasures: National Parks of the World.* Washington, DC: National Geographic Books, 2000, p. 172.
16. Chatwin, *Songlines,* p. 52.
17. Stanley Breeden, "The First Australians," *National Geographic,* February 1988, p. 278.
18. Breeden, "The First Australians," p. 280.
19. Jennifer Westwood, *Mysterious Places.* New York: Barnes and Noble Books, 1987, p. 112.
20. Cowan, *Mysteries of the Dreamtime,* p. 16.
21. Chambers, *A Traveler's History of Australia,* p. 33.

22. Chambers, *A Traveler's History of Australia,* p. 32.

23. Forbes, *Australian Outback,* p. 32.

24. Morgan, *Mutant Message Down Under,* p. 162.

25. Breeden, "The First Australians," p. 286.

26. Singh et al., *Aboriginal Australia,* p. 36.

27. Lambert, *Wise Women of the Dreamtime,* p. 30.

Chapter 3: Family and Community Life

28. Dreaming Online "Indigenous Australia."

29. "Australian Aborigine Culture," 2001. www.allsands.com/History/People/australianabori_ssy_gn.htm.

30. Russel Ward, *The History of Australia: The Twentieth Century.* New York: Harper & Row, 1977, p. 2.

31. Allen L. Johnson. *Australia from the Back of a Camel.* Dayton: Creative Enterprises, 1999, p. 75.

32. Johnson, *Australia from the Back of a Camel,* p. 76.

33. Chambers, *A Traveler's History of Australia,* p. 26.

34. Chambers, *A Traveler's History of Australia,* p. 27.

35. Robert Hughes, *The Fatal Shore.* New York: Random House, 1986, p. 16.

36. Chambers, *A Traveler's History of Australia,* p. 28.

37. Morgan, *Mutant Message Down Under,* p. 46.

38. Quoted in Dreaming Online, "Indigenous Australia."

39. Quoted in Singh et al., *Aboriginal Australia,* p. 93.

40. Chambers, *A Traveler's History of Australia,* p. 30.

41. Roff Smith, *Australia: Journey Through a Timeless Land.* Washington, DC: National Geographic Books, 1999, p. 9.

42. Tim Cahill, *Jaguars Ripped My Flesh.* New York: Vintage Books, 1987, p. 99.

43. Breeden, "The First Australians," p. 279.

Chapter 4: A Clash of Cultures

44. Australian Indigenous Population, "Living Off the Land," www.koori.iisds.com/living./html.

45. Roff Smith, *Australia.* Washington, DC: National Geographic Books, 1999, p. 33.

46. Quoted in Roderick Cameron, *Australia: History and Horizons.* London: Columbia University Press, 1971, p. 37.

47. Keith Kemp, "Pirripaayi: A Case Study of Genocide in Australia," 2000. www.koori.usyd.edu.au/pirripaayi/.

48. Quoted in Ron Fisher, *Wild Shores of Australia.* Washington, DC: National Geographic Books, 1996, p. 15.

49. Linda Christmas, *The Ribbon and the Ragged Square.* New York: Viking Books, 1986, p. 145.

50. Chambers, *A Traveler's History of Australia,* p. 35.

51. Smith, *Australia,* p. 21.

52. Singh et al., *Aboriginal Australia*, p. 49.
53. Quoted in Chambers, *A Traveler's History of Australia*, p. 56.
54. Smith, *Australia: Journey Through a Timeless Land*, p. 8.
55. Hughes, *The Fatal Shore*, p. 7.
56. Bryson, *In a Sunburned Country*, p. 190.
57. Quoted in Johnson, *Australia from the Back of a Camel*, p. 73.
58. Quoted in Hughes, *The Fatal Shore*, pp. 7, 277.
59. Australian Indigenous Population, "Impacts on Aboriginal Life," www.koori.iisds.com/impacts.htm.
60. Quoted in Kemp, "Pirripaayi."
61. Hughes, *The Fatal Shore*, p. 276.
62. Kemp, "Pirripaayi."
63. Bryson, *In a Sunburned Country*, p. 191.
64. Margo Daly et al., *Australia.* London: Rough Guides, 1997, p. 848.
65. Quoted in Hughes, *The Fatal Shore*, p. 417.
66. David Quammen, *Wild Thoughts from Wild Places.* New York: Simon & Schuster, 1998, p. 168.
67. Singh et al., *Aboriginal Australia*, p. 322.

Chapter 5: A White Australia
68. Davidson, *Tracks*, p. 127.
69. Cowan, *Mysteries of the Dreamtime*, p. 91.
70. Smith, *Australia: Journey Through a Timeless Land*, p. 72.
71. Dreaming Online, "Indigenous Australia."

72. Dreaming Online, "Indigenous Australia."
73. Charles Osgood and Barry Peterson. "Look Back at Australia's Government's Attempt to Steal a Generation." *CBS News Sunday Morning,* September 10, 2000.
74. Robert Manne, "The Stolen Generation," 1998. www.tim-richardson.net. misc/stolen_generation.html.
75. Quoted in Manne, "The Stolen Generation."
76. Quoted in Singh, *Aboriginal Australia*, p. 25.
77. Osgood and Peterson, "Look Back."
78. Quoted in Manne, "The Stolen Generation."
79. Quoted in Bryson, *In a Sunburned Country*, p. 271.
80. Bryson, *In a Sunburned Country*, p. 189.
81. Chatwin, *Songlines*, p. 78.
82. Australian Indigenous Population, "Aboriginal Assimilation," www.koori.iisds.com/assimilation.htm.
83. Singh, *Aboriginal Australia*, p. 318.
84. Australian Indigenous Population. www.koori.iisds.com
85. Terry McCarthy, "The Stolen Generation," *Time,* October 2, 2000.
86. Bryson, *In a Sunburned Country*, p. 189.

Chapter 6: Aboriginal Life in Modern Australia
87. Quoted in Michael Christie, "Multicultural Australia Casts Racial Shadow Abroad," *Reuters,* August 25, 2001.

88. Daly et al., *Australia,* p. 57.

89. Quoted in Paul Theroux, *The Happy Isles of Oceania.* New York: Ballantine Books, 1992, p. 61.

90. Quoted in Singh et al., *Aboriginal Australia,* p. 37.

91. Quoted in Morgan, *Mutant Message Down Under,* p. 35.

92. Quoted in Singh et al., *Aboriginal Australia,* p. 47.

93. Quoted in Karen Kissane, "A Young Aborigine," *Time International,* May 20, 1991.

94. Ken Edwards, "Law," *Time International,* April 20, 1992.

95. Theroux, *The Happy Isles of Oceania,* p. 71.

96. Davidson, *Tracks,* p. 177.

97. Quoted in Suganthi Singarayar, "Entrenched Racisms Is Subtle but Pervasive," *Inter Press Service: English News Wire,* August 20, 2001.

98. Christmas, *The Ribbon and the Ragged Square,* p. 144.

99. Cowan, *Mysteries of the Dreamtime,* p. 44.

100. Christmas, *The Ribbon and the Ragged Square,* p. 144.

101. Davidson, *Tracks,* p. 60.

102. Quoted in Singh et al., *Aboriginal Australia,* p. 35.

103. Michael Schaper, "Australia's Aboriginal Small Business Owners," *Journal of Small Business Management,* July, 1, 1999.

104. Davidson, *Tracks,* p. 98.

105. Quoted in Kissane, "A Young Aborigine."

Chapter 7: Hope for the Future

106. John Pilger, "Australia's Black Secret," *New Statesmen and Society,* June 7, 1996.

107. McCarthy, "The Stolen Generation."

108. Quoted in Singh et al., *Aboriginal Australia,* p. 111.

109. Singh et al., *Aboriginal Australia,* p. 75.

110. Carl Robinson, *Australia.* New York: Odyssey Publications, 1999, p. 26.

111. Quoted in National Geographic editors, *Enduring Treasures,* p. 190.

112. Singh et al., *Aboriginal Australia,* p. 59.

113. Dreaming Online, "Indigenous Australia."

114. "Resistance." www.upstarts.net.au/site/ideas/landrights/landrights_resistance.html.

115. Quoted in Smith, *Australia: Journey Through A Timeless Land,* p. 57.

116. Quoted in Dreaming Online, "Indigenous Australia."

For Further Reading

John C. Caldwell, *Let's Visit Australia.* London: Burke Publishing, 1965. This book contains much information about the Aborigines.

Kate Darian-Smith, *Exploration into Australia.* Parsippany, NJ: New Discovery Books, 1995. An excellent book that looks at the various explorers and their experiences in Australia.

Kate Darian-Smith and David Lowe, *The Australian Outback and Its People.* London: Wayland Publications, 1994. An outstanding book that focuses on the Outback region of Australia and the people who live there.

Robert Darlington, *Australia.* Austin, TX: Raintree Steck-Vaughn, 2001. This recently published book offers an excellent look at the continent of Australia and its people.

John Erbacher and Sue Erbacher, *Aborigines of the Rainforest.* New York: Cambridge University Press, 1991. The authors are documentary film producers who have worked with the Kuku Yalanji people in northern Queensland. An excellent look at life among this group of Aborigines.

Ann Heinrichs, *Australia.* New York: Children's Press, 1998. An outstanding book that looks at all facets of Australian life, including a wealth of information about the Aborigines.

Michael Martin, *Children of the World: Australia.* Milwaukee: Gareth Stevens Publishing, 1988. This book looks at the various children of Australia and examines life there from the children's point of view.

Richard Nile, *Australian Aborigines.* Austin, TX: Raintree Steck-Vaughn, 1993. The author grew up in several different Aborigine cultures, and he presents an excellent look at many different tribes.

Jan Reynolds, *Down Under—Vanishing Cultures.* San Diego: Harcourt Brace Jovanovich, 1992. An excellent source about the Aborigines and their difficulties in modern Australia.

April Pulley Sayre, *Australia.* Brookfield, CT: 21st Century Books, 1998. A good overview of the continent and its people.

Al Stark, *Australia: A Lucky Land.* Parsippany, NJ: Dillon Press, 1997. Focuses on Australia and its various peoples.

Works Consulted

Books

Bill Bryson, *In a Sunburned Country.* New York: Broadway Books, 2000. The author is a well-known travel writer. This book is a comprehensive look at Australia and its people as the author journeys throughout the country.

Tim Cahill, *Jaguars Ripped My Flesh.* New York: Vintage Books, 1987. This book by an editor-at-large for *Outside* magazine contains a series of essays, including one about the Dreamtime.

Roderick Cameron, *Australia: History and Horizons.* London: Columbia University Press, 1971. While somewhat outdated, this book does present some good information about early contacts with the Aborigines.

John H. Chambers, *A Traveler's History of Australia.* New York: Interlink Books, 1999. An outstanding reference that contains a great deal of information about the history of the Aborigines along with the development of Australia as an independent nation. A very good source about nearly every facet of Australian history and society.

Bruce Chatwin, *The Songlines.* New York: Penguin Books, 1987. The author ventures into the Outback to learn the meaning of the Aborigines' Songlines.

Linda Christmas, *The Ribbon and the Ragged Square.* New York: Viking Books, 1986. The author spent most of a year traveling through Australia and talking with its inhabitants. A good look at racism.

James Cowan, *Mysteries of the Dreamtime: The Spiritual Life of Australian Aborigines.* New South Wales: Unity Press, 1989. Presents an excellent look at the spiritual life of the Aborigines, including information about the Dreamtime, medicine men, paintings, and the Aboriginal relationship to the land.

Margo Daly et al., *Australia.* London: Rough Guides, 1997. This travel book contains a lot of information about the Aborigines. An excellent reference.

Robyn Davidson, *Tracks.* New York: Vintage Books, 1980. This book is about the author's solo journey across the Australian Outback.

Miriam Estensen, *The Quest for the Great South Land.* New York: St. Martin's Press, 1998. Describes the voyages of the Dutch, Portuguese, British, and others and their contacts with the Aborigines.

Roger Few, *The Atlas of Wild Places.* New York: Facts On File, 1994. This book has a chapter about the Kimberley region and the rock paintings that are found there.

Ron Fisher, *Wild Shores of Australia.* Washington, DC: National Geographic Books, 1996. An outstanding look at Australia's coastline. It includes some excellent information about the Aborigines of Arnhem Land and Tasmania.

Scott Forbes, *Australian Outback.* Singapore: Discovery Communications, 2000. This Insight book, a travel guide through the Outback, focuses on traveling through that region of Australia and gives a great deal of information about the original inhabitants, the Aborigines.

James Harpur, *The Atlas of Sacred Places.* New York: Henry Holt, 1994. This book focuses on more than thirty different sacred sites worldwide, including temples, tombs, pyramids, and natural formations that are considered sacred. There is an excellent section on the Olgas, a sacred place for the Aborigines.

Tony Horowitz, *One for the Road.* New York: Vintage Books, 1987. The author hitchhiked through the Australian Outback and describes his encounters with its inhabitants.

Robert Hughes, *The Fatal Shore.* New York: Random House, 1986. An excellent book about the exploration and settlement of Australia, including the effect this had on the indigenous people.

Allen L. Johnson, *Australia from the Back of a Camel.* Dayton, OH: Creative Enterprises, 1999. The author recounts his adventures as he traveled through the Australian Outback with his grandchildren.

Johanna Lambert, *Wise Women of the Dreamtime.* Rochester, VT: Inner Traditions International, 1993. A collection of Aboriginal myths presented by Aboriginal women.

Marlo Morgan, *Mutant Message Down Under.* New York: Harper Perennial, 1991. Although now identified as fiction to protect the identity of Morgan's Aboriginal guides and to conceal the location of sacred places, the book was originally published in 1994 as a true account of the author's remarkable travels through the Australian Outback with a group of Aborigines. Morgan's work contains a tremendous amount of insight about the Aborigines, presented in a way that allows readers to draw their own conclusions.

National Geographic editors, *Beyond the Horizon: Adventures in Faraway Lands.* Washington, DC: National Geographic Books, 1992. This book contains a chapter about life in the Kimberley region of Australia and its people.

————, *Enduring Treasures: National Parks of the World.* Washington, DC: National Geographic Books, 2000. This book has a long chapter on Australia and some of its national parks.

Bruce Northam and Brad Olsen, *In Search of Adventure.* San Francisco: Consortium of Collective Consciousness, 1997. A compilation of stories, including one about bush tucker.

David Quammen, *Wild Thoughts from Wild Places.* New York: Simon & Schuster, 1988. This book contains a series of essays by the author, another *Outside* editor-at-large, including an excellent one about the Aborigines of Tasmania.

Carl Robinson, *Australia.* New York: Odyssey Publications, 1999. A comprehensive look at the continent that includes a good deal of information about the Aborigines.

Sarina Singh et al., *Aboriginal Australia and the Torres Strait Islanders.* Melbourne: Lonely Planet Publications, 2001. An outstanding reference that focuses exclusively on the indigenous people of Australia and covers their history, struggles, and problems of today. Taking each area of the country, the authors describe the different tribes of Aborigines that still occupy Australia today. Most of the writing is done by Aborigines.

Roff Smith, *Australia*. Washington, DC: National Geographic Books, 1999. This book contains a wealth of information about Australia and focuses on travel throughout the country.

———, *Australia: Journey Through a Timeless Land*. Washington, DC: National Geographic Books, 1999. This is a wonderful book about Australia with dramatic pictures and excellent text about the continent and its people.

Paul Theroux, *The Happy Isles of Oceania*. New York: Ballantine Books, 1992. This well-known author and traveler focuses on Oceania and Australia. The book contains several essays about Australia and the Aborigines.

Russel Ward, *The History of Australia: The Twentieth Century*. New York: Harper & Row, 1977. This book, while somewhat dated, contains information about the Aborigines and their experiences and problems in the twentieth century.

Jennifer Westwood, *Mysterious Places*. New York: Barnes and Noble Books, 1987. A look at some of the world's unexplained symbolic sites, ancient cities, and lost lands, with good information on Uluru.

Periodicals

Harvey Arden, "Journey into Dreamtime," *National Geographic,* January 1991. This excellent article focuses on the Aboriginal Dreamtime and the efforts of modern Aborigines to pursue this traditional spiritual path.

Stanley Breeden, "The First Australians," *National Geographic,* February 1988. An outstanding look at the Aborigines, their lives in the past, and their lives in modern Australia.

Michael Christie, "Multicultural Australia Casts Racial Shadow Abroad," *Reuters,* August 25, 2001. An objective look at racism by an "outsider," or non-Australian, journalist.

Eleni Dimmler and Rachel Nowak, "18 Cathy Freeman." *U.S. News and World Report,* August 20, 2001. A look at Cathy Freeman and her Olympic experience.

John Dunn, "Australia Two Hundred Years Later," *Time,* September 21, 1987. A look at Australia before its bicentennial celebration.

The Economist, "The Aboriginal Patterns that Haunt Australia," April 19, 2000. Looks at the racism that still exists in Australia today.

The Economist, "A Sorry Tale," September 9, 2000. A look at racism.

Ken Edwards, "Law," *Time International,* April 20, 1992. The author discusses the alarming numbers of Aborigines brought to trial and imprisoned.

Encyclopedia of Australia, "Aboriginal Links with the Land," January 1, 1999. This article looks at the importance of land to the Australian Aborigines and how the loss of that land affected their cultural and spiritual lives.

Mark Hodges. "Online in the Outback," *Technology Review,* April 1, 1996. This article looks at the video teleconferencing of the Outback and how it has brought families and communities together.

Robert Hughes, "The Summer Olympics," *Time,* September 11, 2000. A look at Cathy Freeman's victory in the 2000 Summer Olympics and the impact on Australian society, along with a discussion of the problem of racism.

Karen Kissane, "A Young Aborigine," *Time International,* May 20, 1991. The author focuses on the experiences of young Aborigines in prison.

Terry McCarthy, "The Stolen Generation," *Time,* October 2, 2000. The author does an excellent job of presenting the history of those Aboriginal children taken from their parents and forced to assimilate into white society.

Charles Osgood and Barry Peterson, "Look Back at Australia's Government's Attempt to Steal a Generation," *CBS News Sunday Morning,* September 10, 2000. This excellent interview presents testimony from some of the Aborigines of the "Stolen Generation" and their experiences as children.

Michael Parfit, "Australia: A Harsh Awakening," *National Geographic,* July 2000. Examines the threats to wildlife in Australia and the Aborigines' role in preventing further extinctions.

John Pilger, "Australia's Black Secret," *New Statesman and Society,* June 7, 1996. An objective look at racism by a non-Australian journalist.

John Raedler, "Australia Again Examining Aboriginal Laws and Customs," *National Public Radio,* October 18, 1995. This radio show talks about the effects of white society on many of the Aborigines' laws and customs.

Barbara Rudolph, "Behavior: In the Outback Town of Alice Springs," *Time International,* September 24, 1990. This article looks at racism and the problems that Alice Springs' Aborigines face.

Michael Schaper, "Australia's Aboriginal Small Business Owners," *Journal of Small Business Management,* July 1, 1999. This is an excellent article that discusses the problems faced by Aborigines interested in opening small businesses.

Suganthi Singarayar, "Entrenched Racism Is Subtle but Pervasive," *Inter Press Service: English News Wire,* August 20, 2001. A look at the racism that exists in Australia of the twenty-first century.

Claire Smith, "Art of the Dreaming," *Scientific American Discovering Archaeology,* March/April 2000. This informative article looks at the rock art that is ever present in Australia and how the art reflects the traditional practices of the Dreamtime.

Daniel Williams, "Person of the Year: Cathy Freeman," *Time International,* December 25, 2000. A look at Cathy Freeman.

Belinda Wright and Stanley Breeden, "Living in Two Worlds," *National Geographic,* February 1988. This excellent article looks at an Aboriginal family as they struggle to live both a traditional and a modern life in Australia.

David Yeadon, "Journey into Dreamtime," *National Geographic Traveler,* January/February 1995. Focuses on traveling through the Outback and following some of the Aborigines' Songlines.

Internet Sources

"Australian Aborigine Culture," 2001. www.allsands.com/ History/People/australianabori_ssy_gn.htm. A brief synopsis of Aboriginal culture.

Ron Cherry, "Australian Aborigines," June 1993. www.bugbios. com/ced1/aust_abor.html. Focuses on insects as a part of the Aboriginal diet and their use in Aboriginal medicine.

Dreaming Online, "Indigenous Australia." www.dreamtime. net.au/indigenous/timeline3.cfm. An outstanding website that offers a great deal of information about the Aborigines as written by the Aborigines. It includes sections on background information, cultural heritage, the role of storytelling, spirituality, family, the land, social justices, and several timelines tracing Aboriginal history from the earliest of times to the twenty-first century.

James Q. Jacobs, "Down Under History Takes Giant Leap," 1996. www.jqjacobs.net/writing/downundr.html. A good resource for Aboriginal history and the Aborigines' first contact with Europeans.

David Jensen, "The Universe of the Aborigine." http://astronomy. pomona.edu/archeo/australia/australia4/australia4.html. A look at the spirituality and myths of the Aborigines.

Keith Kemp, "Pirripaayi: A Case Study of Genocide in Australia," 2000. www.koori.usyd.edu.au/pirripaayi/. A complicated presentation that concentrates on racism, the assimilation process, and the steady eradication of Aborigines around the Sydney area of Australia.

Robert Manne, "The Stolen Generation," 1998. www.tim-richardson. net/misc/stolen_generation.html. An excellent essay by author Robert Manne about the "Stolen Generation" of Aboriginal children.

Julie Patterson and Julanna Hennessy, "Aboriginal Resistance," April 1999. www4.tpgi.com.au/2juls/resistance.html. Looks at guerrilla efforts and resistance against white encroachment on Aboriginal lands.

"Resistance." www.upstarts.net.au/site/ideas/landrights/landrights_ resistance.html. Focuses on resistance efforts and guerrilla campaigns by Aborigines against white settlers.

Website

Australian Indigenous Population, www.koori.iisds.com. This is an extensive and well-done website that contains a wealth of information about the Aborigines who live in the Northern Territory of Australia. It includes sections on Aboriginal history, living off the land, social control, impacts on Aboriginal life, self-determination, Aboriginal assimilation, Aboriginal land rights, cultural resilience, Aboriginal population, and Aboriginal outstations.

Index

Picture Credits

Cover Photo: © Penny Tweedie/CORBIS
© AFP/CORBIS, 66
© A.P., Australian Department of Information, 35
© ArtToday, 38
© Associated Press, AP, 91
© Baci/CORBIS, 80
© Bettmann/CORBIS, 21
© CORBIS, 43
© COREL Corporation, 33
© Leonardo de Selva/CORBIS, 56
© Eye Ubiquitous/CORBIS, 69, 84
© Hulton Archive, 15, 30, 32, 52, 60, 78
© Zen Icknow, CORBIS, 72
© Chris Jouan 9, 13, 86
© Charles and Josette Lenars/CORBIS, 26
© North Wind, 49
© Reuters NewMedia Inc./CORBIS, 90
© Paul A. Souders/CORBIS, 41
© David and Peter Turnley/CORBIS, 82
© Penny Tweedie/CORBIS, 10, 16, 39, 45, 65, 75

About the Author

Anne Wallace Sharp has written magazine articles and three books for young readers. She is the author of *Daring Women Pirates* and two books in the Lucent Books' Indigenous People of North America series—*The Inuit* and *The Blackfeet.* She is also the author of the adult book *Gifts,* a compilation of stories about hospice patients and their families. A freelance journalist and historian, Anne enjoys reading anything and everything, traveling, and spending time with her two grandchildren, Jacob and Nicole. She lives in Beavercreek, Ohio.